酒店英语阅读（上）

Hotel English Reading & Knowledge

主　编　王向宁

编　委　张董娟　胡特赐　张艳妍　张伟才
　　　　崔新会　杨　静　刘利强

主　审　〔美〕David Goodsell

北京大学出版社
PEKING UNIVERSITY PRESS

图书在版编目(CIP)数据

酒店英语阅读. 上/王向宁主编. —北京：北京大学出版社，2014.10
(21世纪旅游英语系列教材)
ISBN 978-7-301-24977-2

Ⅰ.①酒…　Ⅱ.①王…　Ⅲ.①饭店－英语－阅读教学－高等学校－教材　Ⅳ.①H319.4

中国版本图书馆CIP数据核字(2014)第234169号

书　　　　名：	酒店英语阅读(上)
著作责任者：	王向宁　主编
责 任 编 辑：	初艳红
标 准 书 号：	ISBN 978-7-301-24977-2/H·3610
出 版 发 行：	北京大学出版社
地　　　　址：	北京市海淀区成府路205号　100871
网　　　　址：	http://www.pup.cn　新浪官方微博:@北京大学出版社
电　　　　话：	邮购部 62752015　发行部 62750672　编辑部 62759634　出版部 62754962
电 子 信 箱：	alice1979pku@126.com
印　刷　者：	北京大学印刷厂
经　销　者：	新华书店
	787毫米×980毫米　16开本　7印张　150千字
	2014年10月第1版　2014年10月第1次印刷
定　　　　价：	28.00元

未经许可，不得以任何方式复制或抄袭本书之部分或全部内容。
版权所有，侵权必究
举报电话：010-62752024　电子信箱：fd@pup.pku.edu.cn

ACKNOWLEDGEMENTS

The aim of this textbook is to introduce Hotel English and professional knowledge and skills to Chinese readers and students. We are indebted to many sources for the passages and pictures selected for reading. With regard to the issue of copyright, we have made extensive efforts to contact the publishers and authors of these passages and pictures, but for various reasons we have been unable to establish communication in some cases. In these cases we apologize to the publishers and authors in advance and will be happy to make fuller acknowledgement in due course. For any questions concerning copyright and permissions, please contact.

E-mail: willarr@126.com

We will be happy to make any necessary arrangements for the appropriate settlement of any possible copyright issues.

前　言

《酒店英语阅读》是北京市教委教育教学改革促进项目的成果之一，是面向全国高等院校旅游专业、酒店管理专业、英语专业学生编写的专业英语类教材，同时也可供旅游、酒店行业从业人员作为自学教材和参考用书。

本套教材力图在框架布局、内容选材、版块设计等方面做出特色和创新，填补相关领域的空白，在高校教育教学改革中做出有益的尝试，并考虑到目前教学的特点，努力做到内容丰富、语言地道、版面轻松活泼、版块多样，突出实用性、针对性和趣味性。

本套教材分为上、下两册。上册内容主要介绍"酒店行业知识"，下册内容涵盖"酒店实际运营"的各个方面。"酒店行业知识"从宏观角度系统地介绍了酒店业态、酒店分类、特色酒店、酒店评级、酒店集团、酒店管理名校、服务礼仪、酒店发展前景与面临的挑战。"酒店实际运营"则从微观角度介绍了酒店内前厅、客房、餐饮、康乐、招聘培训、市场营销、安全保卫、处理投诉等内容。

本套教材每个单元由七个版块构成：1）Lead-in 导读：引导读者了解单元主题信息；2）Reading 阅读：包含3篇阅读文章，从不同角度、不同侧面介绍单元主题内容，并配有注释及精美图片；3）Useful Words and Expressions 实用词汇与表达：从文中选取重要短语及表达，方便读者学习；4）Practical Reading 实用文体欣赏：引入酒店中常用的招聘广告、菜单、酒水单、预订表、规章制度、促销广告等，拓宽读者视野，熟悉业内常用文体形式；5）Knowledge 趣味小知识：补充一些行业小知识，增强阅读趣味性；6）Exercises 练习：包含 Phrase Translation（短语翻译）和 Passage Translation（段落翻译），旨在加强语言技能训练的同时，从不同侧面丰富单元主题覆盖面；7）Case Study 案例分析：这个版块多选用酒店业界的经典案例，例如著名酒店管理集团创始人故事、酒店实际运营相关案例等，让读者了解案例所渗透出的酒店管理与服务理念，以提高读者分析和解决问题的能力，起到举一反三的启迪作用。

本教材在编写过程中，参考了一些出版物和网站（详见参考文献）。由于选材广泛，书中没有一一注明出处，希望得到原作者的支持和谅解，并接受我们诚挚的谢意！此外，为了使学生有直观、感性的认识，并使版面活泼轻松，我们采用了一些公开发表的图片。由于部分

酒店英语阅读(上)

图片无法联系到原作者,所以敬请原作者和读者见谅!

  本教材在编写过程中,承蒙中瑞酒店管理学院实训基地九十余家酒店相关人员的帮助,承蒙瑞士洛桑酒店管理学院咨询顾问Alexia, Chen Weicheng, Linda的指导,承蒙迪拜卓美亚酒店管理学院John Fong的帮助,承蒙本院实习学生的协助,承蒙外籍专家David Goodsell, Leo(Liu Zhigang)在语言上的把关,承蒙中瑞酒店管理学院科研管理中心在配套资金上的鼎力支持,在此表示衷心感谢!

  本教材由北京第二外国语学院中瑞酒店管理学院教授王向宁担任主编,参与编写人员为:张董娟、胡特赐、张艳妍、张伟才、崔新会、杨静、刘利强。

  鉴于时间仓促、编者水平有限,本教材难免有疏漏、不足之处,欢迎广大读者批评指正。

王向宁
2014.7

Contents

Unit 1　Hotel and Careers ·· 1
　　Lead-in 导读 ·· 1
　　Reading 阅读 ··· 2
　　　　Text A　About the Hotel ··· 2
　　　　Text B　About the Hotel Industry ···································· 4
　　　　Text C　Working in the Hotel Industry ·························· 6
　　Useful Words and Expressions 实用词汇与表达 ················· 7
　　Practical Reading 实用文体欣赏 ·· 8
　　Knowledge 趣味小知识 ··· 9
　　Exercises 练习 ·· 10
　　Case Study 案例分析 ··· 11

Unit 2　Hotel Classification ·· 12
　　Lead-in 导读 ·· 12
　　Reading 阅读 ··· 13
　　　　Text A　Hotel Categories ·· 13
　　　　Text B　Resort Hotel ··· 15
　　　　Text C　Budget Hotel ·· 17
　　Useful Words and Expressions 实用词汇与表达 ··············· 19
　　Practical Reading 实用文体欣赏 ·· 19
　　Knowledge 趣味小知识 ··· 20
　　Exercises 练习 ·· 21
　　Case Study 案例分析 ··· 22

Unit 3　Unique Hotels ··· 24
　　Lead-in 导读 ·· 24

酒店英语阅读（上）

    Reading 阅读 ·············· 25
        Text A   Poseidon Undersea Resorts ·············· 25
        Text B   Hotel de Glace — A Delicate Ice Hotel ·············· 27
        Text C   Whitepod Hotel in Switzerland ·············· 28
    Useful Words and Expressions 实用词汇与表达 ·············· 30
    Practical Reading 实用文体欣赏 ·············· 31
    Knowledge 趣味小知识 ·············· 31
    Exercises 练习 ·············· 32
    Case Study 案例分析 ·············· 34

Unit 4   Hotel Ratings ·············· 36

    Lead-in 导读 ·············· 36
    Reading 阅读 ·············· 37
        Text A   Chinese Hotel Rating System ·············· 37
        Text B   American Hotel Rating System ·············· 38
        Text C   British Hotel Rating System ·············· 40
    Useful Words and Expressions 实用词汇与表达 ·············· 42
    Practical Reading 实用文体欣赏 ·············· 42
    Knowledge 趣味小知识 ·············· 43
    Exercises 练习 ·············· 44
    Case Study 案例分析 ·············· 45

Unit 5   Hotel Groups ·············· 47

    Lead-in 导读 ·············· 47
    Reading 阅读 ·············· 48
        Text A   Shangri-La Hotel Group ·············· 48
        Text B   InterContinental Hotel Group ·············· 50
        Text C   Hilton Hotel Group ·············· 52
    Useful Words and Expressions 实用词汇与表达 ·············· 54
    Practical Reading 实用文体欣赏 ·············· 54
    Knowledge 趣味小知识 ·············· 55
    Exercises 练习 ·············· 56
    Case Study 案例分析 ·············· 57

Unit 6　Schools and Education　58
- Lead-in 导读　58
- Reading 阅读　59
  - Text A　Cornell University-School of Hotel Administration　59
  - Text B　Lausanne Hotel School — EHL　61
  - Text C　Glion Institute of Higher Education　62
- Useful Words and Expressions 实用词汇与表达　64
- Practical Reading 实用文体欣赏　65
- Knowledge 趣味小知识　65
- Exercises 练习　67
- Case Study 案例分析　68

Unit 7　Etiquette and Service　70
- Lead-in 导读　70
- Reading 阅读　71
  - Text A　Proper Serving Etiquette　71
  - Text B　Chinese Table Manners　72
  - Text C　Keys to Delivering Good Service　74
- Useful Words and Expressions 实用词汇与表达　75
- Practical Reading 实用文体欣赏　76
- Knowledge 趣味小知识　77
- Exercises 练习　78
- Case Study 案例分析　79

Unit 8　Development and Issues　80
- Lead-in 导读　80
- Reading 阅读　81
  - Text A　E-hospitality　81
  - Text B　Green and Sustainability　83
  - Text C　Future Development　84
- Useful Words and Expressions 实用词汇与表达　86
- Practical Reading 实用文体欣赏　86
- Knowledge 趣味小知识　87

Exercises 练习 ·· 88
Case Study 案例分析 ·· 89

练习参考答案 ·· 90
参考书目 ··· 99

Unit 1　Hotel and Careers

▶▶ Lead-in 导读

　　"酒店"一词来源于法语,最初意为贵族在乡间招待贵宾的别墅,后来又称为宾馆、旅馆、旅店、旅社、商旅、客店、客栈等。现在的酒店,除主要为客人提供住宿服务外,还提供餐饮、游戏、娱乐、购物、商务、宴会、会议等服务与设施。本单元就酒店的定义、发展历史、酒店业职业特点等方面进行简要概述。

Reading 阅 读

Text A

About the Hotel

What Is a Hotel?

When most people think about "hotels,"① they think about buildings containing guest rooms for sleeping. In its narrowest sense, this definition may be correct. However, today's travelers have a wide variety of lodging alternatives, and the definition just cited is of limited use. For example, at one extreme, a person may choose a lavish destination resort in an exotic location that, in addition to sleeping rooms, offers many recreational alternatives, food and beverage outlets, and numerous other amenities. Other

travelers prefer a full-service hotel② that offers, in addition to sleeping rooms, a variety of food and beverage services. These may include ala carte dining rooms, coffee shops, or lounges, and room service and banquet facilities. Still other travelers desire a limited-service hotel③ that simply provides sleeping rooms with no food and beverage outlets. Besides, facilities other than those commonly referred to as hotels may offer sleeping accommodations. These include private clubs, casinos, cruise ships etc. In addition, there are unique hotels such as those that consist only of suites (known as all-suite hotels) and those designed to attract guests who tend to stay for a long time (extended-stay hotels).④

Vocabulary
cite *v.* 引用
lavish *adj.* 奢华的
exotic *adj.* 异国的
recreational *adj.* 娱乐的
amenity *n.* 便利设施
ala carte 自己点菜,零点菜
lounge *n.* 大堂酒吧
banquet *n.* 宴会
census *n.* 人口普查

The History of Hotel

Evidence of hotels and the hospitality industry have been recorded as far back as biblical times when Mary and Joseph arrived in Bethlehem during the census. As the Bible depicts, Mary and Joseph were refused accommodations because there "was no room

at the inn." Since the beginning of time, people have traveled for commerce, religion, family, health, immigration, education and recreation.

As cited by Texas Tech University, the word "hospitality" comes from the Latin root meaning "host" or "hospice." The university further noted that the first hotels were nothing more than private homes opened to the public. Most, unfortunately, had poor reputations. Under the influence of the Roman Empire, inns and hotels began catering to the pleasure traveler[5] in an effort to encourage visitors.

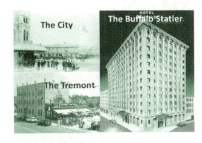

The first inn located in America was recorded in the year 1607 and lead the way with many other firsts in the hospitality industry. The first publicly held hotel (the City Hotel) opened in New York in 1792. The first modern hotel (the Tremont) opened in Boston in 1829 and the first business hotel (the Buffalo Statler) opened in 1908.

From there, a surge of hotels flooded American and the rest of the world, with prominent names such as Radisson, Marriott and Hilton.

root *n.* 词根
Radisson 雷迪森
Marriott 万豪
Hilton 希尔顿

Notes

1. 《旅游饭店星级的划分及评定》(国家旅游局,2010)给出旅游饭店(Tourist Hotel)的定义:以间(套)夜为单位出租客房,以住宿服务为主,并提供商务、会议、休闲、度假等相应服务的住宿设施,按不同习惯可能也被称为宾馆、酒店、旅馆、旅社、宾舍、度假村、俱乐部、大厦、中心等。
2. full-service hotel 全服务酒店,指提供全套服务的酒店,包含各式餐厅、宴会厅等。
3. limited-service hotel 有限服务酒店。国际上将没有宴会和餐饮的酒店统称为有限服务酒店。
4. In addition, there are unique hotels such as those that consist only of suites (known as all-suite hotels) and those designed to attract guests who tend to stay for a long time (extended-stay hotels).除此之外,还包括只由套房组成的全套房酒店以及专供长住客人的延时居住酒店。
5. pleasure traveler 同 leisure traveler,休闲旅客。

Text B

About the Hotel Industry

Hotel Industry

The hotel industry is a sector of business that revolves around① providing accommodations for travelers. Success in the hotel industry relies on catering to the needs of targeted clientele, creating a desirable atmosphere, and providing a wide variety of services and amenities. The management of hotels has grown from its modest roots in providing the bare essentials of lodging into a large, multi-faceted, and diverse industry②.

The hotel industry is undergoing many changes. The demand for hotels is affected as the economic fortunes of countries, regions, and cities rise and fall③. Each year, companies and hotels change ownership and new companies and brands enter the marketplace. Brand names that are popular today may not be around in the next decade. For example, Renaissance Hotels of Hong Kong acquired Stouffer Hotels (formerly a U.S.-based company) from the  Nestlé Corporation of Switzerland, and converted all of the Stouffer hotels into Renaissance hotels, which were then acquired by Marriott International. The Stouffer hotel name no longer exists.

As you can see, the hotel industry is a global industry. InterContinental Hotels, headquartered in London, operates hotels in 100 countries and territories; the French company Accor has hotels in 92 countries; Marriott International has hotels in 67 countries; and U.S.-based Starwood Hotels & Resorts has hotels in 95 countries.

Hospitality Today

What is the hospitality industry? This is not an easy question, and books on the subject offer many different answers. Some view the hospitality industry as comprising four sectors: lodging, food, entertainment,

Vocabulary
clientele n. 客户
Renaissance 万丽
InterContinental 洲际
Accor 雅高
Starwood 喜达屋

and travel. However, usually the hospitality industry is viewed as encompassing mainly lodging and food service businesses. If we define the industry this way, we can include such facilities as school dormitories, nursing homes, and other institutions.

The Hospitality Industry		
Lodging Operations	Food Service Operations	Other Operations
All-suite hotels	Commercial cafeterias	Airlines
Casino hotels	Education food service	Campgrounds
Conference centers	Employee food service	City clubs
Full-service hotels	Full-service restaurants	Country clubs
Limited-services hotels	Health-care	Cruise ships
Resorts	Lodging food service	National parks
Retirement communities	Quick-service restaurants	
	Recreational food service	
	Social caterers	

encompass *v.* 包含
campground *n.* 露营场所
caterer *n.* 餐饮供应者
inevitable *adj.* 必然的

Continued expansion of the lodging industry is inevitable. No one knows precisely how many new hotels and other lodging properties will be built in the next decade, or where most of them will be located. All that can be said with certainty is that ④ career opportunities in lodging will continue to grow.

Notes

1. **revolve around** 围绕
   e.g. Debate will therefore revolve around voting rights. 因此，争论将围绕投票权展开。

2. The management of hotels has grown from its modest roots in providing the bare essentials of lodging into a large, multi-faceted, and diverse industry. 酒店管理已经从最初仅提供基本住宿服务发展成为一个大规模、多方位、多样化的行业。bare essentials 基本必需品。

3. The demand for hotels is affected as the economic fortunes of countries, regions, and cities rise and fall. 对酒店的需求随着国家、地区、城市的经济发展起伏而变化。rise and fall 涨落，起伏。

4. All that can be said with certainty is that ... 唯一能够确定的是……

Text C

Working in the Hotel Industry

Why do people go into the hospitality industry? If you were to ask people who have spent their careers in this business what they like most about it, you would get a wide variety of answers. Some of the most popular are:

● **The industry offers more career options than most.** No matter what kind of work you enjoy, and wherever your aptitudes lie, there is a segment of the industry that can use your talents.

● **The work is varied.** Because hotels and restaurants are complete production, distribution, and service units, managers are involved in a broad array of activities①.

● **There are many opportunities to be creative.** Hotel and restaurant managers might design new products to meet the needs of their guests, produce training programs for employees, or implement challenging advertising, sales promotion, and marketing plans②.

● **This is a "people" business.** Managers and supervisors spend their workdays satisfying guests, motivating employees, and negotiating with vendors and others.

● **Hospitality jobs are not nine-to-five jobs**③. Hours are highly flexible in many positions. (Some see this as a disadvantage, however.)

● **There are opportunities for long-term career growth.** If you are ambitious and energetic, you can start with an entry-level job and move up. The industry is full of stories of people who started as bell persons or cooks and rose to high management positions, or opened their own successful businesses.

● **There are perks associated with many hospitality jobs.** If you become the general manager of a resort, you can dine in its restaurants with your family and friends, and use its recreational facilities. Airline and cruise employees get free or reduced-fare travel.

Despite these advantages, there are some aspects of the business that many people don't like:

Vocabulary
aptitude *n.* 天资, 才能
vendor *n.* 供应商, 小贩
perk *n.* 额外待遇, 小费
reduced-fare *adj.* 打折的

● **Long hours.** In most hospitality businesses, the hours are long. The 40-hour workweek is not the norm, and 50- to 60- hour workweeks are not unusual.

● **Nontraditional schedules.** Hospitality managers do not work a Monday-through-Friday schedule. In the hospitality field you will probably often find yourself working when your friends are relaxing.

● **Pressure.** There are busy periods when managers and employees are under intense pressure to perform.

● **Low beginning salaries.** Entry-level jobs for management trainees tend to be low-paying compared to some other industries④.

norm *n.* 标准，基准

Notes

1. Because hotels and restaurants are complete production, distribution, and service units, managers are involved in a broad array of activities. 由于酒店和餐厅是完整的生产、流通、服务单元，因此管理者要参与到广泛的活动当中。
2. implement challenging advertising, sales promotion, and marketing plans 实施有竞争力的广告、促销活动和营销计划。
3. Hospitality jobs are not nine-to-five jobs. 酒店的工作并非朝九晚五。
4. Entry-level jobs for management trainees tend to be low-paying compared to some other industries. 与其他行业相比，酒店业管理培训生的初级职位通常工资较低。

Useful Words and Expressions 实用词汇与表达

1. in its narrowest sense 狭义上讲
2. at one extreme 在一个极端
3. nothing more than 不过是
4. revolve around 围绕
5. all that can be said with certainty is that... 唯一能够确定的是……
6. go into 加入
7. be involved in 参与到，涉及
8. a broad array of 广泛的
9. under intense pressure 在强压之下
10. compared to... 与……相比

Practical Reading 实用文体欣赏

ALCOHOLIC DRINKS
Whiskey $7.90
Gin $7.60
Vodka $8.00
Tequila $8.30
Cognac $6.75
Beer $5.50

Wine and cocktails also available

SOFT DRINKS
Cola $4.25
Lemonade $3.50
Mineral water $4.25

HOT BEVERAGES
Espresso $5.40
Filter coffee $5.30
Tea $4.90
Hot chocolate $5.80

SNACKS
Potato chips $1.00
Assorted nuts $2.00

Unit 1 Hotel and Careers

Knowledge 趣味小知识

迪拜帆船酒店

迪拜帆船酒店,又称阿拉伯塔酒店(Burj Al Arab Hotel),是世界上第一家7星级酒店。它是迪拜的新标志,也是阿拉伯人奢侈的象征。阿拉伯塔最初的创意是由阿联酋国防部长、迪拜王储阿勒马克图姆提出,最终由英国设计师汤姆·赖特(Tom Wright)设计。酒店建于海滨人工岛之上,形似塔状建筑,共56层,高达三百多米,拥有202套复式客房,其中位于25层的780平方米的总统套房奢华非凡,房费高达每晚1.8万美元。酒店拥有

八辆宝马和两辆劳斯莱斯,专供住店客人直接往返机场,当然客人也可从28层专设的停机坪坐直升机,空中俯瞰迪拜美景。

但是,依照酒店业评级标准,并不存在7星一说,那为什么帆船酒店会得此殊荣呢?原来,早在酒店开业之初,一位英国女记者就入住于此,她感受到了前所未有的服务质量。回国以后,她就在报纸上美言盛赞帆船酒店的豪华奢侈和优良服务。"我已经找不到什么语言来形容它了,只能用7星级来给它定级,以示它的与众不同。"从此以后,这个免费广告就传遍了整个世界。

酒店房型

酒店的客房因不同的分类标准而划分为不同的类型。最常见的分类标准有以下几种:根据单间客房所配置床的种类和数量分类,分为单人间、大床间、三人间、双床间(包括标准间、家庭房等);根据构成套房的房间数量及内部装潢布置的档次分类,分为普通套房、商务套房、行政套房、豪华套房、总统套房;根据客房的位置分类,分为内景房、外景房(包括市景房、山景房、海景房等)、相连房

酒店英语阅读（上）

和角房；根据特殊人群或需求分类的房型有残疾人客房、盲人客房、无烟房、女性客房、老年人客房等。其中，单人间（Single Room）、标准间（Standard Room）、高级房（Deluxe Room）、商务房（Business Room）和行政房（Executive Room）为基本房型。每家酒店的客房类型包含其中一种或多种，酒店星级越高，客房越豪华，拥有的套房数量也越多。

Exercises 练习

1. Phrase Translation

1) 有限服务酒店
2) 全套房酒店
3) 商务酒店
4) 总经理
5) 管理培训生
6) wine label
7) ala carte
8) extended stay hotels
9) entry-level jobs
10) rise and fall

2. Passage Translation

Passage A

The hospitality industry is the largest and one of the most dynamic in the world today. It offers boundless possibilities in an exciting field in which new areas are opening up every day. Hospitality calls on a multitude of different talents, including both business savvy and artistic creativity. It allows you to develop your own combination of skills and interests and to find a position corresponding to your own unique profile. Because of its wide range of business activities and specializations, hospitality also allows you change fields easily within the industry. You can shift direction as your interests change and grow, with plenty of flexibility to follow new trends and opportunities and to keep up with rapid technological developments. You can also use your expertise to launch your own company or original business concept.

Passage B

20世纪80年代中国饭店开始走向转型期，最具代表性的当属知名的建国饭店。它是首家中外合资的饭店，建于1982年，由半岛酒店集团管理。同时期还有其他一些著名的饭店，如北京兆龙饭店。这是一家由香港船王包玉刚捐赠给中国的五星级饭店。引人注目的是，邓小平出席了盛大的开业典礼，并亲自用中国书法为酒店题名。

Case Study 案例分析

Thomas Keller

Every once in a while a new chef bursts on the scene who captures the imagination of the entire restaurant industry worldwide. Thomas Keller is one of those people. His restaurant, The French Laundry, has been named the best restaurant in the world by Restaurant Magazine. Bon Appetit, Esquire, Gourmet, and Zagat have all named it the best restaurant in America. Time has picked him as America's best chef. Located in Yountville, California, in the Napa Valley, The French Laundry has five stars from the Mobil Travel Guide. Another restaurant of Keller's, Per Se, has three Michelin stars——the only restaurant in all of Manhattan with that ranking.

Keller was born at Camp Pendleton, Oceanside, California, in 1955, the son of a Marine drill instructor. Eventually the family settled in Palm Beach, Florida, where Keller spent his teenage years.

In his cookbook, The French Laundry Cookbook, Keller explains his philosophy. "When you acknowledge, as you must, that there is no such thing as perfect food, only the idea of it, then the real purpose of striving toward perfection becomes clear: to make people happy. That's what cooking is all about. But to give pleasure, you have to take pleasure yourself. For me it's in the satisfaction of cooking every day, the mechanical jobs I do daily, year after year."

Keller clearly is a perfectionist. He tells his readers, "Cooking is not about convenience and it's not about shortcuts. The recipes in this book are all about wanting to take time to do something priceless. Take your time. Take a long time."

So what does Keller do at the French Laundry that is so innovative? To begin with, his cooking is characterized by small portions served slowly over a long period of time. Some diners finish their meals in two and a half hours, others take four.

Another thing Keller wants you to be thinking is that the $210 bill per person (including service) is worth every penny. The fact that the restaurant is typically booked three or four months in advance is all the proof that is needed that it is.

Thinking:
1. What does Keller do at the French Laundry that is so innovative?
2. What are some common reasons for restaurant failure?

Unit 2   Hotel Classification

▶▶ Lead-in 导读

酒店种类繁多,划分标准不一。一般来说,酒店的分类标准包括:地理位置、规模大小、服务等级和目标市场。本单元首先介绍酒店的分类情况,之后选取以提供休闲娱乐为主、发展势头强劲的度假型酒店和在国内市场占据重要地位的经济型酒店进行详细介绍。

Unit 2 Hotel Classification

Reading 阅 读

Text A

Hotel Categories

Hotels vary in location, size, function, and cost. There are many criteria for classifying hotels based upon different factors. Some general factors are as follows:
- Location
- Size of property
- Level of service
- Target market

Location

Some of the most generally recognized hotel-location categories are: center-city, suburban, resort, highway, airport and motels.

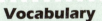

● **Center-City Hotels** are located in the heart of the city. Tariffs are high due to their location advantage as these hotels are near corporate offices, shopping arcades, business centers, etc. Normally business clients are preferred and it has a high occupancy on week days.

● **Suburban Hotels** have very quiet surroundings as they are located in suburban areas; their occupancy characteristic is generally having high traffic on the weekend. Tariffs of these hotels are reasonably low, therefore, they are perfect for budget travelers.

Vocabulary
property n. 财产
category n. 分类
suburban adj. 城郊的
tariff n. 收费, 费用
occupancy n. 占用; 入住
benchmark n. 基准
mega adj. 巨型; 超大型

Size of Property

The benchmark for the categorization of hotels is on the number of rooms available in the hotel.①

● **Small Hotels** are the hotels that have less than 300 rooms.
● **Medium Sized Hotels** are the hotels that have 300-600 rooms.
● **Large Hotels** are hotels that have more than 600 rooms.
● **Mega Hotels** are hotels that have more than 1000 rooms.

13

酒店英语阅读（上）

Level of Service

This is the most important criterion for classifying hotels. Hotels can be categorized into budget hotels, mid-market or semi budget hotels, upscale hotels and luxury hotels. This is done on the basis of the level of service they offer.

mid-market *adj.* 中档的
upscale *adj.* 高档的
concierge *n.* 礼宾
prime *adj.* 主要的
celebrity *n.* 名人
kitchenette *n.* 小厨房

- **Mid-market Hotels** offer small living rooms with appropriate furniture and small bed rooms. The facilities include a swimming pool, health club, etc.

- **Luxury Hotels** provide world class service to the guest. These hotels have a variety of restaurants, lounges, concierge service, shopping arcade, sports facility, etc. The prime market for these hotels is mainly celebrities, business men, corporate heads and high ranking political figures.

Target Market

The hotels based on target market include all-suite hotels, apartment hotels, timeshare hotels, convention hotels, casino hotels, etc.

- **All-Suite Hotels** are designed for executives and families who will pay for upscale living or work space.② Some form of Kitchenette may be found but the new suite hotels tend to provide full service as well as recreational or fitness amenities and a variety of conference and meeting rooms.

- **Convention Hotels** have a large convention complex and cater to people attending a convention or conference.

Notes

1. The benchmark for the categorization of hotel is on the number of rooms available in the hotel. 这种分类以酒店拥有的客房数量为标准来划分。

2. All-Suite Hotels are designed for executives and families who will pay for upscale living or work space. 套房型酒店是为那些愿意为高档奢华的生活或工作环境买单的公司高管及富裕家庭所设计的。

Text B

Resort Hotel

Introduction

People may have various reasons for going to a resort, but the primary reason to take a holiday from the cares and worries of work is to enjoy entertainment and relaxation in a changed location. Popular locations commonly include beaches, mountains, lakes, deserts, tropical islands, and others beautiful sites. Typically, these sites are spacious, offering outdoor recreation facilities and sports such as skiing, boating, tennis, and golf.

Although the vacation market has long been — and still is — the favorite group of the majority of resorts, many resorts have placed a stronger emphasis on soliciting conventions, corporate meeting, and incentive groups in order to survive in today's competitive hospitality business environment. Larger resorts provide excellent convention and meeting facilities and, in particular, are able to attract more meeting business because of the combination of vacation and business services they offer.

Vocabulary
primary *adj.* 首要的,主要的
tropical *adj.* 热带的
spacious *adj.* 宽敞的,广阔的
solicit *v.* 征求,恳求
incentive *adj.* 激励的
overlapping *adj.* 重叠的
ranch *n.* 大牧场

Types of Resorts

Resorts may be classified under various categories, with some overlapping categories. Popular types of resorts include (but are not limited to) the following:

By seasonality:		
Year-round resort	Summer resort	Winter resort
By designation:		
Spa resort	Golf resort	Ski resort
Guest ranch	Diving resort	Fishing resort

Casino resort	Conference resort	Camp-site
Eco resort①	Theme park resort	
By location:		
Urban resort	Beach or seaside resort	Lake resort
Mountain resort	Island resort	Desert resort
Tropical rain-forest resort	Farm-related	
By size:		
Mega-resort	Boutique resort	
By form of ownership:		
Conventional	Timeshare②	Condo resort③
Vacation club	Luxury destination club	
Others:		
All-inclusive resort④	Mixed-used resort	Themed/fantasy
Floating (cruise ships)		

Operating Challenges

Many guests travel considerable distances to resorts. Consequently, they tend to stay longer than at transient hotels. This imposes numerous special challenges, including the way guestrooms are designed. Extra space needs to be allocated for storage of both the guest's personal effects and the house provisions. In addition, recreation, entertainment, area attractions, shopping, spas, and other amenities should be available to add to guest satisfaction.

considerable *adj.* 大量的
transient *adj.* 热带的
allocate *v.* 分配, 指定
attentive *adj.* 留意的, 专心的
cyclical *adj.* 周期的, 循环的
stimulate *v.* 刺激, 激励

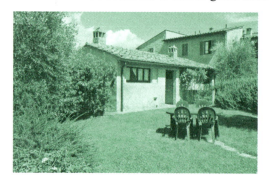

The challenge to the food and beverage manager is to provide quality menus that are varied and are presented and served in an attractive, attentive manner. To achieve this, resorts often use a cyclical menu that repeats itself every fourteen to twenty-one days. Also, they provide a wide variety and number of dishes to stimulate interest.

Notes

1. Eco-resort 生态旅游，即以有特色的生态环境为主要景观的旅游，其内涵更强调对自然景观的保护，是可持续发展的旅游。
2. Timeshare 分时度假，即将酒店或度假村的一间客房或一套旅游公寓的使用权分成若干个周次，以会员制的方式一次性出售给客户，会员获得每年到酒店或度假村住宿7天的一种休闲度假方式。
3. Cando resort 公寓式酒店，指以公寓形式存在的酒店套房。其特点在于：其一，它类似于公寓，有居家的格局和良好的居住功能；其二，它配有全套家具与家电，能够为客人提供酒店的专业服务，如室内打扫、床单更换及一些商务服务等。
4. All-inclusive resort "全包"套餐式度假村，即购买套餐时包含机票、酒店住宿、餐饮、娱乐等一切旅游开支，在其酒店（度假村）内可以随便享用其食品及设施。

Text C

Budget Hotel

Definition

A budget hotel, called a "bed & breakfast" hotel in Western countries, offers standardized hotel services with a better performance ratio than luxury hotels, because it consists of only a high-standard accommodation facility. It has no accessory facilities for meetings, entertainment and catering, and cuts down on procurement costs and staff through standardized brand operation and facility management.

History

It was not until the 1960s that the first budget hotels were introduced—Motel 6 ① in California, Days Inn ② in Georgia, and La Quinta ③ in Texas. Sam Barshop, founder of La Quinta, explained his idea this way: "We have a very simple concept. What we're doing is selling beds. Not operating restaurants, not running conventions-just selling beds." By eliminating the restaurants, and the lobby and meeting space that Holiday Inns offered, La Quinta and other budget properties were able to offer Holiday Inn-type rooms at 25 percent less. Some chains, like Motel 6, sold

Vocabulary
accessory *adj.* 附属的，辅助的
procurement *n.* 采购

rooms for as low as $6. They were able to offer such low prices by using modular and prefabricated construction materials and choosing less-than-ideal locations, where land costs were lower. These chains offered hardly any amenities at all. In the early days, some had a coin slot in their guestroom television sets for pay-as-you-view TV!

prefabricated *adj.* 预制构件的
less-than-ideal *adj.* 不太理想的
meager *adj.* 微薄的
debut *n.* 开张
respectively *adv.* 分别地
saturation *n.* 饱和

In China

Compared with developed countries, the budget hotel industry started late in China. The proportion of budget hotels is less than 30% in China's hotel industry, while it has exceeded 70% in the U.S. The development space of the budget hotel in China is broad.

With the participation of other enterprises and foreign brands, the competition in the budget hotel industry is fiercer. The budget hotel industry has entered an era of meager profit.

After a debut and continuous expansion, by the first half of 2012, the number of budget hotels in China has reached 8,313, and the number of room has reached 837,220, growing 360 times and 257 times respectively compared with 2000.

At present, the number of budget hotel brands is 419. The market share of Home Inns Group, Hanting Inns and Hotels and 7 Days Group Holdings has reached more than 47%. Compared with the second and third-tier cities, the number of budget hotels in Beijing, Shanghai, Guangzhou and some other first-tier cities has reached saturation. Many hotels are exploring markets in the second and third-tier cities, which is a trend in the industry.

Notes

1. Motel 6 6号汽车旅馆。1962年创建于美国加利福尼亚州,在美国和加拿大共有1000多家酒店,是一家主要的经济型连锁酒店。
2. Days Inn 戴斯酒店。"戴斯"是温德姆酒店集团(WyndhamWorldwide)旗下最大、最著名的酒店品牌,1970年创立至今已有超过40年历史。
3. La Quinta 拉昆塔酒店

Unit 2 Hotel Classification

Useful Words and Expressions 实用词汇与表达

1. vary in 在……方面有差异
2. be categorized into 归类于
3. as follow 如下列各项
4. on the basis of 根据,基于……
5. cater to 迎合,投合
6. place an emphasis on 把重点放在……
7. be located in 位于,坐落于
8. explore the market 拓展市场
9. tend to 趋于做……
10. enter an era of 进入一个……时代

Practical Reading 实用文体欣赏

Special Promotion

Inclusions:
- Two-night accommodation in Superior room
- Breakfast buffet for two days
- One time Asian set lunch or dinner with 5 courses or Western set with 4 courses. Dinner or lunch date is at the guest's choice at time of check-in.
- No supplement of child, sharing the bedding with their parents
- Free two mineral water bottles
- Free Wi-Fi connection
- Free use of Health and Recreation Center
- Free return airport transfer

RMB 1888

Valid from 15 August - 31 Oct 2014
— subject to room availability
— not applicable on Public Holidays

酒店英语阅读（上）

Knowledge 趣味小知识

酒店试睡员

"酒店试睡员"在国外被称为"酒店品评家"，被网友称作"史上最爽职业"。其基本工作为试睡酒店：体验酒店的服务、环境、卫生、价格、餐饮等多个方面，比如床垫软硬、空调冷暖、网速快慢、下水道是否畅通、淋浴水流是否过大等等，调查后根据自己的感受写成报告，交给公司后在网上发布，为众多网友提供借鉴。此外还需要收发、回复用户信件或问题，不定期接受媒体采访；维护个人博客，分享第一手酒店图片与影片等。

试睡员的工作看似简单，但需要大量的时间和精力。他们不仅要不断发掘新的酒店，试睡前做大量准备工作，还必须对酒店的种种细节进行细致入微的观察，并用大量的文字、图片和视频来描述自己的住宿体验。因此，热情、理性、敏锐的观察力与感受力、周全的思考力、缜密的思维、扎实的文字功底，以及热爱旅游、乐于分享所见所闻、敢于尝试新事物的冒险精神等都是成为一个合格酒店试睡员的基本要求。待遇方面根据行业现有标准执行，月薪最高可达万元。

酒店收费方式

一般说来，国际上星级酒店通行的收费方式有以下五种，即：

● 欧洲式（European Plan，简称EP）：只包括房费，而不包含任何餐费的收费方式，为世界上大多数酒店采用。

● 美国式（American Plan，简称AP）：不但包括房费，而且还包括一日三餐的费用，因此，又被称为"全费用计价方式"，多为远离城市的度假型酒店或团队客人所采用。

● 修正美式（Modified American Plan，简称MAP）：包括房费和早餐，除此以外，还包括一顿午餐或晚餐(二者任选一个)的费用。这种收费方式较适合于普通旅游客人。

● 欧洲大陆式(Continental Plan,简称CP):包括房费及欧陆式早餐(Continental Breakfast)。欧陆式早餐主要包括冷冻果汁、烤面包、咖啡或茶。

● 百慕大式(Bermuda Plan,简称BP):包括房费及美式早餐(American Breakfast)。美式早餐除了包含欧陆式早餐的内容以外,通常还包括鸡蛋和火腿或香肠或咸肉等肉类。

Exercises 练习

1. Phrase Translation

1) 目标市场
2) 客户满意度
3) 二三线城市
4) 投币式电视
5) 市场份额
6) performance ratio
7) transient hotel
8) procurement costs
9) budget traveler
10) shopping arcade

2. Passage Translation

Passage A

Convention hotels usually range in size from about 350 to more than 2,000 rooms, with ample public spaces and meeting facilities to support the rooms. Up-to-date audiovisual and communications technology and large-scale food and beverage capabilities are requirements for the convention hotel. Newer convention hotels tend to devote about twice the normal space to meeting rooms and include more public space for handling group check-ins than do typical classic hotel. The logistics of human traffic in convention hotel may be managed somewhat differently from a classic hotel. For example, separate registration areas may be designated for independent guests and for convention guests to not only increase traffic efficiency, but to reduce noise and congestion in the lobby as well. Likewise, vehicular traffic for independent and convention guests may be channeled into separate parking zones.

Passage B

分时酒店是使用权很特殊的一种酒店。这些酒店通常拥有一些客房或度假型公寓单元。它们的使用权按照10至40年甚至更长的期限被分成若干个周次,以会员制的方式出售给客户。会员获得每年7天的使用权。会员可以通过交换服务系统把自己的使用权与其他地区的会员进行交换,以此降低去各地旅游度假的成本。

Online Review

Olivia Plaza Hotel is a four-star luxury hotel located on Plaza Catalunya, and the top of the world famous La Rambla in Barcelona. The hotel has modern rooms with elegant and superior-quality finish.

Ricardo Samaan, Revenue Manager at Olivia Plaza Hotel, considers online reviews to be a fundamental part of doing business as a hotel in today's internet influenced economy. "There are more and more people who read online reviews in detail, and these people have a very clear idea of what they will find in our hotel when they arrive." Ricardo explains that the hotel used to look at reviews about once a month, but he realized this was not enough to stay on top of guest comments.

Ricardo believes monitoring and reacting to online reviews on a daily basis is critical today. "Thanks to the internet, our clients have a lot more influence than they had a few years ago. The hotel market is very competitive, and clients now have the possibility to compare contrasting information and opinions of past clients of our hotel. The result is that they know exactly what to expect they are booking and what they will find at hotel when they get there."

Over the last year, Olivia Plaza Hotel received 930 online reviews across 15 different sources. The company has more online reviews than any of their direct competitors, so monitoring online reviews on a regular basis is key for the hotel's success.

Ricardo checks his alerts and logs into the ReviewPro tool daily to read the latest reviews and monitor the hotel's performance over time. He looks at the hotel's general performance by Global Review IndexTM, a score ReviewPro developed to enable hotels to measure their overall online reputation, and at Departmental Indexes for service, gastronomy and cleanliness. He also looks at ReviewPro's online review Tracking that allows him to see the latest guest reviews individually and access any specific review with a single click, giving him the opportunity him to quickly respond to a given review if needed. "Thanks to ReviewPro, we know on a daily basis if the service and cleanliness match a guest's expectations, so we can react quickly if needed."

Thinking:
1. Do you think the online review is important for the hotel business, why?
2. What will you do when you receive the online reviews of guest's complaint?

Unit 3　Unique Hotels

▶▶ Lead-in 导读

人们对于浪漫、自然、新奇的追求导致了众多独具特色酒店的应运而生。这些酒店通常具有独特的设计元素和环境特点。本单元特别选取了斐济波塞冬海底度假酒店、加拿大魁北克冰酒店、瑞士阿尔卑斯山圆屋生态酒店三个酒店以领略特色酒店的独特魅力。

Unit 3 Unique Hotels

Reading 阅 读

Text A

Poseidon Undersea Resorts

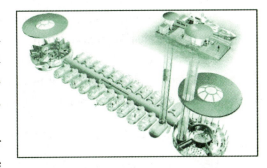

The Poseidon Undersea Resorts① in Fiji is the world's first seafloor resort and it is built in a lagoon of crystal clear water near a private island named Poseidon Mystery. The hotel of this resorts is located 40ft underwater and covers an area of 5,000 acres.

In the resorts, guests access their underwater suites through an elevator. They can enjoy the undersea views in their suite, and even interact with the marine life in the proximate environment and feed the fish around their suite

Suite Construction

Measuring 10m x 5.1m each, the undersea suites in Poseidon are built as detachable stand-alone modules. Nearly 70% of each suite's surface is encased with acrylic plastic, a material which is strong and remarkably transparent, providing vacationers with spectacular views of the undersea coral gradens. The resort's design takes full advantage of acrylic's ability to maximize visibility while maintaining structural soundness.

Service and Facilities

Poseidon provides all the comforts, conveniences and opportunities that only a five-star resort can offer. Services available include two fine dining establishments, one on land and one below the sea, presenting plates of culinary excellence day and night. A dive shop and a retail boutique will also be at the guests' service, along with a library, a lounge, a theater, a conference room and a wedding chapel. Fitness amenities include a executive golf course, tennis courts, private splash pools and a fitness center.

Vocabulary

seafloor n. 海底
lagoon n. 环礁湖
detachable adj. 可拆分的
stand-alone adj. 独立的
encase v. 包住；围绕
acrylic n. 丙烯酸（塑料）
visibility n. 能见度
culinary adj. 烹饪的
chapel n. 小教堂

酒店英语阅读（上）

Poseidon and the Environment

The Poseidon Undersea Resorts is more than a resort. It is a life-changing experience, a celebration of nature's wonders, and an illustration of responsible behavior towards the environment. All around Poseidon Mystery Island, an unspoiled tropical marine ecosystem awaits the visitors. A specific program, Poseidon Coral Reef Sanctuary Project②, has been designed to prevent negative impacts on the environment. Advanced coral farming and propagation techniques are utilized to encourage the development of biodiversity.

Safety

The structure of Poseidon Undersea Resorts is designed to meet the structural requirements applicable to a submarine pressure hull.③ Each individual component of the complex will be automatically isolated in the highly unlikely event of a structural breach. Every unit has a safety dome with an entrance hatch where professionally trained divers can enter. Diving staff regularly practice rescue procedures in a purpose-built unit.④

unspoiled *adj.* 未损坏的
propagation *n.* 繁殖
biodiversity *n.* 生物多样性
dome *n.* 圆屋顶
purpose-built *adj.* 特制的

Notes

1. The Poseidon Undersea Resorts 波塞冬海底度假村，位于斐济群岛共和国，是目前世界上第一个海底度假村，游客可以在距离海平面40英尺以下的奢华环境中度过浪漫优雅的假日。

2. Poseidon Coral Reef Sanctuary Project 波塞冬珊瑚礁保护区项目。在波塞冬海底度假村的建设和运行过程中尽力保存和保护周边礁石区的珊瑚。

3. The structure of the Poseidon Undersea Resorts is designed to meet the structural requirements applicable to a submarine pressure hull. 波塞冬海底度假村的结构设计能够满足水下耐压壳体的特殊结构要求。

4. Diving staff regularly practice rescue procedures in a purpose-built unit. 度假村的潜水员定期在一处专门建造的区域进行营救演练。

Text B

Hotel de Glace — A Delicate Ice Hotel

Hotel de Glace① is the first and only ice hotel in North America, and is built each December for an opening date in early January. Made of snow and ice, once the guests step into the hotel, it feels like they are wandering in a crystal palace. And with delicate artistic designs and carvings, they may also wonder if they are in a pure art gallery.

The hotel is located 5km north of Quebec City, on the first slopes of the Laurentian Mountains, in the Charlesbourg borough. ② It has a three-month lifespan each year before being brought down in April. The hotel has been described as a "tourist hotpot", given the fact that nearly one million people have visited it so far.

Construction

The hotel takes about a month and a half to build with 50 workers. It makes its own snow using a special mixture to adjust the humidity. It is built with metal frames and allowed to harden for a few days, at which point the cranes are removed. ③ The hotel is made of 30,000 tons of snow and 500 tons of ice, and the walls are up to four feet thick to keep the temperature inside low enough. It is usually made (the architecture and size may vary from season to season) in arches of 5 meters over rooms, and larger and higher spaces for a grand hall, a chapel, a bar and a grand ice slide. And due to its constantly rebuilding, the design of the hotel changes every year.

Rooms and Amenities

The hotel had 11 double beds when it was first opened in 2001. Now there are 51 double beds, all made of ice with a solid wood base and comfortable mattress. ④ When the time comes, a cozy sleeping bag, an isolating bed sheet and a pillow are delivered to the rooms. Only the bathrooms are heated and located in a separate insulated structure. While all furniture is made of ice, the guests also can have

Vocabulary

gallery *n.* 画廊；走廊
slope *n.* 斜坡
borough *n.* 自治市镇
lifespan *n.* 寿命
crane *n.* 起重机
arch *n.* 拱形
mattress *n.* 床垫；褥子
cozy *adj.* 舒适的
insulated *adj.* 保暖的

酒店英语阅读（上）

drinks and cocktails in ice glasses and take a bath in indoor heated washrooms or outdoor hot tubs.

tub *n.* 浴盆
ceiling *n.* 天花板

Weddings

The Hotel de Glace has been described as one of the "10 dream wedding locations." ⑤ White weddings don't come much whiter than at this Ice Hotel. Everything is made of ice, including a spectacular chapel, which has ceilings resembling a small cathedral. Till now, over 300 weddings have been celebrated in the chapel since its first opening.

Notes

1. Hotel de Glace 原名为法语 Hôtel de Glace, 意为冰酒店。
2. The hotel is located 5 km north of Quebec City, on the first slopes of the Laurentian Mountains, in the Charlesbourg borough. 酒店位于加拿大魁北克市北面5公里处劳伦山脉第一道山坡查尔斯堡镇。
3. It is built with metal frames and allowed to harden for a few days, at which point the cranes are removed. 它是由金属框架构建，结冰坚固几天后，撤去起重机。
4. Now there are 51 double beds, all made of ice with a solid wood base and comfortable mattress. 现有51张双人床，皆为冰制，上为实木床板，再铺以舒适的床垫。
5. The Hotel de Glace has been described as one of the "10 dream wedding locations." 冰酒店被称为"世界十大梦想婚礼地"之一。

Text C

Whitepod Hotel in Switzerland

Whitepod Hotel is a luxury eco-hotel in Switzerland located in the Swiss Alps. ①Combining pristine beauty and irreplaceable luxury, it is placed 1,700 meters above the sea level, which enable the guests to enjoy the views of the stunningly beautiful Alps.② Isolated from all urban pollution, the mountain region lends itself beautifully to such an eco-tour.

The Pods

Whitepod Hotel has a collection of 15 geodesic dome pods, each of which covers an area of 40 square meters. All pods are

Vocabulary

pristine *adj.* 原始的
geodesic *adj.* 网格球顶的

placed on large wooden platforms serving partially as terraces with chairs and tables. They are equipped with high quality insulation coupled with a simple wood burning stove, an arrangement which keeps in-house guests comfortably warm in winter and cool in summer. Each pod sleeps up to 4 and is individually decorated. It has a large cozy double bed for 2 people and a mezzanine where the beds are more appropriate for children from 8 to 16 years. It contains a fully equipped bathroom with shower, toilet and sink directly hooked up to a private water source. The pods are lit by lanterns.

Features

The appearance of the pods changes with the season, white in winter and green during the summer, depending on the color of the canvas it is covered with, in order to blend inconspicuously with the surrounding landscape. To ensure the guests can steal a glimpse of the snowy mountain tops from any of the pods, large windows are set facing the valley. What's more, there is a special additional pod facing Lake Geneva③. Among the pods, the guests can see a chalet that features a spa and sauna as well as a dining area. Besides eating at the restaurant, they can also dine in the pods.

Activities

Guests can enjoy numerous activities when stay in the Whitepod Hotel. Various hikes and dog sledding trips are organized, both of which can be with or without a guide. One of the most adventurous activities is hang gliding, which lasts about 45 minutes.④ For skiing, there are two private ski lifts and 7km of ski slopes are reserved just for the guests. As soon as they put on snowshoes, a journey of wonder opens to them.

Vocabulary

stove n. 火炉
mezzanine n. 夹楼
sink n. 下水道
canvas n. 帆布
inconspicuously adv. 难以察觉地
glimpse n. 一瞥；一看
chalet n. 瑞士山中小屋
sledding n. 乘雪橇
gliding n. 滑翔

酒店英语阅读（上）

Eco-Friendly

Whitepod is an extremely environmentally conscious construction.⑤ Using the pods, it offers a low-impact accommodation in an untouched and pristine alpine environment. The pods were built of local and recycled materials and the waste is recycled. To minimize the effect the guests generate, the number of the guests and the daily water and electricity consumption are also limited. There, all measures are employed to preserve the natural world and every opportunity is taken to help guests embrace nature to the full, whether through the breathtaking views from the pods, or out on expeditions.

low-impact adj. 环保的
breathtaking adj. 令人激动的

Notes

1. Whitepod Hotel is a luxury eco-hotel in Switzerland located in the Swiss Alps. 圆屋酒店是位于瑞士阿尔卑斯山上的一家豪华生态酒店。
2. Alps 阿尔卑斯山。它位于欧洲中心的山脉，覆盖意大利北部边界、法国东南部、瑞士、列支敦士登、奥地利、德国南部及斯洛文尼亚。
3. Lake Geneva 日内瓦湖。为著名的风景区和疗养地，是阿尔卑斯湖群中最大、最著名的一个。
4. One of the most adventurous activities is hang gliding, which lasts about 45 minutes. 其中最惊险刺激的活动之一是45分钟的悬挂滑翔。
5. Whitepod is an extremely environmentally conscious construction. 圆屋酒店的建筑极为体现环保意识。

Useful Words and Expressions 实用词汇与表达

1. be encased with 被……包住
2. interact with 与……互动
3. take full advantage of 充分利用
4. be due to 由于
5. bring down 打倒，推倒
6. coupled with 外加，加上
7. hook up to 连接到
8. be equipped with 配备有
9. blend with 与……融合、协调
10. to the full 充分地，完全地

Unit 3 Unique Hotels

Practical Reading 实用文体欣赏

ABC Hotel

540.853.8295
Reservations Required

Our Signature Massage
1 Hour $110   90 Minutes $165

Couple's Massage
1 Hour $110   90 Minutes $330

Hand and Foot Care
Manicure $50   Pedicure $60

Hair Styling
Up-do's, Blow-outs or Custom Styling
Starting at $60

Make-up Application
Daytime $60   Evening $70

Facials
Available in-room or en suite
1 hour $110

10 am to 7 pm Monday thru Saturday
Closed Sunday

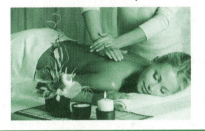

Knowledge 趣味小知识

酒店香氛

　　酒店的香味营销最早在20世纪90年代的国外酒店管理集团或个性化酒店中出现，是根据自身的品牌和独特的客户定位，设计与其相符的"香味标签"，将品牌导入酒店的专属香氛之中，让顾客"闻香识酒店"。酒店选择合适的香味可以提升客人舒适度及满意度，并通过精油挥发有效地改善酒店空间环境，促进住店客人的身心健康。亚太地区最大的豪华酒店集团香格里拉可以说是香味营销方面的典范，他们已有专属的"香格里拉香氛"品牌，是以香

酒店英语阅读（上）

草、檀香和麝香为基调，带有些许佛手柑、白茶和生姜味的别致香气，能够起到安抚和舒缓情绪的功效。威斯汀酒店大堂散发的是一种高雅的白茶香，混合着天竺葵和小苍兰的味道，使人平静、放松。喜来登酒店大堂的香气则混合了无花果、薄荷、茉莉和小苍兰香，让人觉得宾至如归。福朋酒店采用的则是萃取自苹果和桂皮的香气，一闻到它就会使人想起苹果派和酒店朴实的风格。

开夜床服务

开夜床服务(Turn-down Service)是和酒店送餐服务(Room Service)同等重要的服务。开夜床服务可以简单归纳为"进房、开灯、拉窗帘、开夜床、清理杂物、整理浴室、检查、离房"。此项服务一般从晚5:30或6点开始，或按客人要求开始，晚9点之前做完，因为9点以后再敲门势必会打扰客人休息。

开夜床服务的具体流程为：服务员进房后，打开壁灯，拉好窗帘，打开空调调节室温。叠好床罩放在箱架上。将靠近主床头一侧的毛毯连同上面一条床单一起掀起60cm，成45°角。同时打开夜灯，摆好拖鞋。整个操作快速、准确、规范。其后，服务员将更换客人用过的玻璃杯、烟灰缸，倒掉纸篓垃圾，简单擦拭桌面，物品放在规定位置，不翻阅或挪动客人放在桌面上的物品。卫生间客人用过的口杯、烟灰缸、毛巾、浴巾、面巾等用品一起撤出，缺额补齐。简单清理面盆、浴盆、马桶，保持清洁。同时检查客房酒水饮料，开好酒单，补充酒水。整个房间整理遵守操作程序，服务快速、周详。

Exercises 练习

1. Phrase Translation

1）海底度假村
2）海洋生物
3）艺术画廊
6）hook up to
7）interact with
8）in-house guests

4）充分利用
5）再利用材料
9) a glimpse of
10) to the full

2. Passage Translation

Passage A

Kelebek means "the butterfly" in Turkish, it is so called because its two fairy chimneys that rise from the rocks like the wings of a butterfly. Set in the mythical lands of Cappadocia, the rock formations that created the hotel date back to a pre-historical volcanic eruption. For thousands of years, people have lived among these caverns and caves. The earliest mention of the rock villages of Cappadocia is in a Persian text from 6th Century BC. The "Cappadocians" are mentioned in writings by the first historian, Herodotus. Your stay at the Hotel Kelebek allows you to experience the unusual interior of their traditional cave dwellings. You can also select a room that used to house a medieval monk and some rooms contain ancient mosaics. The hotel has all the modern conveniences you need so you can spend your days exploring this fascinating part of the world.

Passage B

美国电锯艺术家(chainsaw artists) Dennis and Frances夫妻经过几年时间的努力，终于建成了另类的"犬吠公园旅馆"（Dog Bark Park Inn），向游客提供住宿和早餐。无论是建筑物的外形还是内部摆设，甚至连食物，都被做成了狗的形状。犬吠公园位于爱达荷州Camas Prairie的中心。两头庞大的"猎兔犬"(Beagles)坐落在公园的绿地之上。一头叫做"斯威特威利"(Sweet Willy)，高达30英尺，建于1997年，另一头叫"托比"(Toby)，12英尺高。起初，这对夫妇建造犬吠公园只是想作为制作、展示和销售电锯雕刻作品的场地。后来，他们决定打造两头"猎兔犬"，并开始以狗为创作主题。"犬吠旅馆"深受爱狗人士的喜爱，慕名而来的客人们通过一个"秘密通道"进入猎兔犬的"身体"，房间中还准备了小狗形状的饼干，十分有趣！

Case Study 案例分析

Back to the Nature with Bubbles

French designer Pierre Stephane Dumas went a step ahead: the hotels he designed in France not only can provide people with a wonderful and unique experience, but also can pack them in and vanish into the thin air, leaving no trace on the ground where it once stood. Does it sound spooky?

The fact that hotels have nowadays become much more than just a place where one can spend a few nights while traveling makes sense. Far from becoming just the destination, they seek to offer the experience—staying there can be something no other place in the world can come close to. Reaching further than just design or boutique hotels, the finest examples of this trend offer their clients not only uncommon services, but also make their stay there memorable, and enjoyable, and leave them yearning for more of it.

Situated in Bouches-du-Rhone (near Marseille), Attrap'Rêves is eco-friendly, cosy and unique, and it is the dream of any enterprising hotelier. Of course, for people who prefer the pampering that luxury hotels offer, this hotel is something very far from it. Actually, they are not the clients Dumas had in mind when designing these bubbles.

Dumas started with the idea of making something light and airy, with no need for complicated construction and permit procedures, in line with nature and the trees.

The bubbles are made by Bubble Tree, a firm making pre-fabricated tents. The sphere maintains its bubble shape thanks to a blower which creates a soft pressure. This pressure avoids moisture problems and allows for air renewal. Therefore, in the bubble, you can have a fresh and healthy atmosphere, without moisture, mosquitoes, dust or allergens.

In Dumas' words, "Climbing up a tree is a natural experience, enjoying spectacular views and soaking in this extraordinary light filtering through the canopy of the trees, outside of typical four walls. In designing the cabin bubble, I wanted to create a special area that can provide unique moments of proximity between man and nature with the lowest environmental impact possible."

The bubble huts are either transparent or half opaque, depending on the amount of privacy one wants to enjoy. They come in various types, like the Zen cabin or the Glamour one, equipped with all necessary furniture and amenities for customers to enjoy their stay under the stars and in the forest. One can even enjoy a jacuzzi in the woods!

Thinking:
1. What are the reasons for the design of Bubble Hotel according to Pierre Stephane Dumas?
2. Why is the hotel so popular?

Unit 4　Hotel Ratings

▶▶ Lead-in 导读

　　为了对外销售客房和方便客人选择,各国政府或旅游业机构均会根据本国酒店的建筑规模、设施设备、服务质量、管理水平等将酒店划分为不同的等级。本单元将介绍一些具有代表性的分级标准,即中国星级酒店评定标准、美国钻石酒店评定标准和英国星级酒店评定标准。

Unit 4 Hotel Ratings

Reading 阅读

Text A

Chinese Hotel Rating System

Star Rating

In order to promote the development of tourism, and protect the interests of tourists, the People's Republic of China implemented its uniform hotel rating system in 1993. In the Chinese rating system, accommodations can be rated as one, two, three, four or five stars according to facilities, scale, service quality and management. Normally, rated acommodations provide better facilities and service than non-rated ones. The National Tourism Administration① is responsible for the implementation of the star-based evaluation throughout the country.

5-Star Rating ★★★★★: These hotels offer only the highest level of accommodation and services. The hotel locations can vary from the very exclusive locations of a suburban area, to the heart of downtown. The hotel lobbies are sumptuous, and the rooms complete with stylish furnishing and quality linens. The hotel amenities often include: VCR's, CD stereos, garden tubs or Jacuzzis, in-room video library, heated pools and more.② Fine restaurant dining, room service③, concierge service④, Fitness Centers and valet and/or garage parking are typically available.

4-Star Rating ★★★★: These are mostly large, formal accommodations with smart reception areas, front desk service and bellhop service. Usually, they are located near accommodations of the same caliber and neighborhood shopping malls, dining areas and other major attractions. The level of service is well above average, and the rooms are well lit and furnished. Restaurant dining, room service, concierge service, Fitness Centers and valet parking and/or garage service are also usually available.

3-Star Rating ★★★: These hotels offer more spacious accommodations that include well appointed rooms and decorated lobbies. They are often located near major expressways or business

> **Vocabulary**
> implement *v.* 实施
> uniform *adj.* 统一的
> accommodation *n.* 旅馆
> evaluation *n.* 评价
> exclusive *adj.* 独有的
> sumptuous *adj.* 奢华的
> caliber *n.* 质量
> expressway *n.* 高速公路

areas, convenient to shopping and moderate to high priced attractions. They provide medium-sized restaurant dining, but room service availability may vary. Valet parking, Fitness Centers and pools are often provided.

2-Star Rating ★★: Tthis rating usually denotes independent and name brand hotel chains with a reputation for offering consistent quality amenities. These hotels are usually small to medium-sized, and are conveniently located to moderately priced attractions. The facilities typically include telephones and TV's in the bedroom.

1-Star Rating ★: These hotels are often 2-4 stories high and usually have a more personal atmosphere. They're usually located near affordable attractions, major intersections and convenient to public transportation. Furnishings and facilities are clean but basic.

reputation n. 声誉
atmosphere n. 氛围
intersection n. 十字路口

Notes

1. The National Tourism Administration 中华人民共和国国家旅游局(简称国家旅游局),英文缩写为NTA, 是国务院主管旅游工作的直属机构。
2. The hotel amenities often include: VCR's, CD stereos, garden tubs or Jacuzzis, in-room video library, heated pools and more. 酒店设施通常包括录像机、音响、花园浴缸或按摩浴缸、室内影院、恒温泳池等。
3. room service 客房送餐服务
4. concierge service 礼宾服务

Text B

American Hotel Rating System

AAA Diamond Rating

Although various associations and corporations maintain their own independent rating systems, the U.S. hotel industry observes no uniform hotel rating system. Perhaps the best-known system among them is the diamond-based ratings of the AAA (American Automobile Association)①.

The AAA system annually evaluates more than twenty-nine thousand accommodations. To become AAA approved, the

Vocabulary
association n. 协会
corporation n. 公司;团体
annually adv. 每年
approve v. 批准;认可

establishment must first meet 27 basic requirements, covering comfort, cleanliness and safety. If it is approved, AAA sends out anonymous raters to evaluate the hotel and assign a diamond rating from one to five②.

AAA does not approve poor quality hotels. All Diamond rated hotels are good hotels—the diamond ratings aren't really intended to mean five diamonds are "better" than four, just that five star hotels are more luxurious. A one-diamond hotel is an economy hotel, but it's a good economy hotel③.

> **Vocabulary**
>
> anonymous *adj.* 匿名的
> budget-minded *adj.* 精打细算的
> enhancement *n.* 提高
> refined *adj.* 精制的
> fundamental *adj.* 基础的
> sophistication *n.* 高雅
> meticulous *n.* 细致的
> impeccable *adj.* 无瑕的

AAA explains its ratings as follows:

One Diamond ♦: Appeal to budget-minded travelers. Provide essential, no-frills accommodations. Meet basic requirements pertaining to comfort, cleanliness and hospitality.

Two Diamonds ♦♦: Appeal to travelers seeking more than basic accommodations. Provide modest enhancements to overall physical attributes, design elements and amenities, typically at a moderate price.

Three Diamonds ♦♦♦: Appeal to travelers with comprehensive needs. Multifaceted with a distinguished style, including marked upgrades in the quality and level of physical attributes, amenities and comfort.

Four Diamonds ♦♦♦♦: Upscale in all areas. Progressively more refined and stylish④. Physical attributes reflect enhanced quality throughout. Fundamental hallmarks include extensive amenities and a high degree of hospitality, service and attention to detail.

Five Diamonds ♦♦♦♦♦: The ultimate in luxury and sophistication. Physical attributes are extraordinary in every manner. Fundamental hallmarks include meticulous service that exceeds guest expectations, impeccable standards of excellence and personalized services⑤ and amenities that provide an unmatched level of comfort.

Notes

1. AAA (American Automobile Association) 美国汽车协会。参与评定星级旅馆和饭店,是美国旅馆和饭店的权威评审机构之一,其每年要对美国、加拿大、墨西哥及加勒比海等地的近5.7万家饭店及旅馆进行评审,其中只有0.26%可以登上"五星"榜。

2. If it is approved, AAA sends out anonymous raters to evaluate the hotel and assign a diamond rating from one to five. 如果得到批准,美国汽车协会将派遣匿名评审员到酒店进行评审,其后将颁发1至5

颗钻石的评定证书。
3. economy hotel 经济型酒店。经济型酒店(Budget Hotel)是相对于传统的全服务酒店(Full Service Hotel)而存在的一种酒店业态，其最大的特点是房价便宜。最早出现在20世纪50年代的美国，如今在欧美国家已是相当成熟的酒店形式。
4. Progressively more refined and stylish. 逐步更加精致和时尚。
5. personalized service 个性化服务

Text C

British Hotel Rating System

Visit Britain Quality Assessments

In Britain, the national assessing bodies like Visit England, Visit Scotland, Visit Wales, Northern Ireland Tourist Board and the AA (Automobile Association)① carry out Quality Assessment. They assess accommodation by the same criteria, and award 1 to 5 stars reflecting facilities and overall quality. The more stars awarded - the higher the level of quality.

Specific types of accommodation need to be assessed in a different way because the 1-5 star rating system covers all kinds of accommodation from campsites, to B&Bs② to city-centre hotels, all offering different levels of facilities and services. But for all accommodation types, there is no advance notice when being assessed③. The assessors stay overnight as 'mystery guests' in all B&Bs and hotels, to give them an opportunity to test aspects of the guest experience such as the welcome, the comfort of the bed, and food and cleanliness.

One star ★: Tend to be smaller, privately owned, properties. Acceptable overall level of quality. Adequate provision of furniture, furnishings and fittings.

Two stars ★★: Tend to be small, privately owned properties, including resort hotels④, Inns and small commercial hotels. Good overall level of quality. All units self-contained - 2 bathrooms, where there are eight or more guests.

Three stars ★★★: A more formal style of hotel, likely to be

Vocabulary
assess v. 评定；评估
criteria n. 标准
provision n. 供应
self-contained adj. 自足的；完备的

Unit 4 Hotel Ratings

larger than one and two star hotels, with a greater range of facilities and services. Good to very good level of quality. Good standard of maintenance and decoration. Ample space and good quality furniture. All double beds with access from both sides. Microwaves.

Four stars ★★★★: More formal service is expected at this level. Excellent overall level of quality. Very good care and attention to detail will be obvious throughout. Either access to a washing machine and drier, if not provided in the unit, or a 24 hour laundry service.

Five stars ★★★★★: Accommodation must be of luxury quality with services to match. Exceptional overall level of quality. High levels of décor, fixtures and fittings, together with excellent standards of management efficiency and guest services. Excellent range of accessories and personal touches.

Awaiting Inspection[5]: An inspection has been applied for by these properties, but they have not yet been inspected or graded by Visit Britain.

microwave *n.* 微波炉
exceptional *adj.* 特别的
décor *n.* 装饰
accessories *n.* 配件
inspection *n.* 检查

Notes

1. Visit England, Visit Scotland, Visit Wales, Northern Ireland Tourist Board and the AA (Automobile Association) 英格兰旅游局、苏格兰旅游局、威尔士旅游局、北爱尔兰旅游局及汽车协会
2. B&Bs 是一种酒店的类型，和民宿相似，全称为 Bed and breakfast，简称为 B&B。主要提供过夜服务及早餐服务。
3. But for all accommodation types, there is no advance notice when being assessed. 不过，无论是哪种类型的酒店，评审前都不会预先接到通知。
4. resort hotels 度假酒店。以接待休闲度假游客为主，为休闲度假游客提供住宿、餐饮、娱乐与游乐等多种服务功能的酒店。
5. Awaiting Inspection 待评审酒店

酒店英语阅读（上）

Useful Words and Expressions 实用词汇与表达

1. be rated as... 被列为……
2. be responsible for... 对……负责
3. vary from 不同于
4. meet...requirements 达到……的要求
5. send out 派遣
6. intend to 打算
7. appeal to 对……产生吸引力
8. exceed...expectations 超出……的期望
9. carry out 施行
10. apply for 申请

Practical Reading 实用文体欣赏

Room Service Menu

Breakfast	Price
Your choice of omelette	$8.50
Yogurt with granola	$8.75
Pancakes with maple syrup	$7.25
Soups and Salads	
Soup of the day	$8.25
Vegetable soup	$8.00
Chef's salad	$11.45
Sandwiches and Burgers	
Chicken club sandwich	$10.55
Classic burger	$10.65
Desserts and Cakes	
Chocolate cake	$7.30
Apple pie	$6.90
Ice cream	$6.00
Beverages	
Coffee	$5.00
Tea	$4.50
Soft drinks	$4.45

Unit 4 Hotel Ratings

Knowledge 趣味小知识

中餐宴会摆台

中餐宴会摆台须根据宴会的性质、形式、主办单位的具体要求、参加宴会的人数、面积等来制订方案。中餐宴会多采用圆台,主人的座位应正对厅堂入口,其视线能纵览全厅。中餐宴会摆台的具体要求如下:

- **台布**　中心凸缝向上,且对准正、副主人,台布四周下垂部分均等。
- **玻璃转盘**　放于圆桌中央,转盘中间放置花瓶。
- **十套餐具**　整体要求合理、整齐、美观。筷架位于骨碟右上方约45°。筷架上近骨碟一侧放长柄汤匙,外侧放筷子。汤碗位于骨碟左上方。汤匙放入碗中,匙柄偏向左上。
- **公筷及公匙**　每桌两副,分别放在主人席和副主人席三杯(250ml水杯、100ml高脚葡萄酒杯、25ml白酒杯)的正前方。
- **水杯、葡萄酒杯、白酒杯**　从左到右依次摆放于骨碟正上方,葡萄酒杯底距骨碟3厘米,水杯底与葡萄酒杯底1.5厘米,葡萄酒杯底与白酒杯底1厘米,三杯中心线成一直线。
- **四只烟缸**　分别摆在正、副主人的右侧和左侧,成正方形。
- **两份菜单**　摆放美观,原则上位置在主人、副主人右侧。

西餐宴会摆台

摆台主要指餐台、席位的安排和台面的摆设。摆台的基本要求是:餐具卫生,图案对正,距离均匀,整齐美观,清洁大方,餐具摆放相对集中,方便客人用餐,同时便于服务员席间为客人提供服务。

西餐宴会需要根据宴会菜单进行摆台,每上一道菜就要换一副刀叉,通常不超过七件,包括三刀、三叉和一匙,摆放时按照上菜

顺序由外到内放置。其具体摆法如下:
- 先将垫盘摆好作为定位,垫盘左边按顺序摆放餐叉、鱼叉、冷菜叉;垫盘右侧按顺序摆放餐刀、鱼刀、冷菜刀,刀刃朝左;
- 前方摆汤匙,汤匙前边交叉摆放点心叉和点心匙;
- 叉的左侧摆面包盘,盘内斜放黄油刀,盘的前方摆黄油碟;
- 点心叉、匙的前方摆水杯、色酒杯、白酒杯。口布折花放在垫盘内或插在水杯中。
- 摆设一席好的台面,能为客人就餐增添舒适高雅的气氛,给客人带来赏心悦目的感受,给宴会增添喜庆隆重的气氛。

Exercises 练习

1. Phrase Translation

1) 酒店等级评定体系
2) 酒店大堂
3) 预先通知
4) 客户体验
5) 服务质量
6) above average
7) hotel amenities
8) moderate price
9) washing machine
10) public transportation

2. Passage Translation

Passage A

Different from the traditional star-rating ones, Boutique Hotels emphasize individuality. Successful ones always have three characteristics, namely, independent spirit, personality traits and cultural heritage. And generally this kind of accommodation boasts both the rich flavor of local culture and a unique historical memory of it. When staying in such accommodations, guests can have unparalleled enjoyment which is lacking in the star-rated hotels. Chinese Courtyard, which is peculiar to China, is a typical quadrangle dwelling as used by ancient Chinese. A courtyard always consists of a central main building and two wing buildings on either side. Recently, more and more courtyards have converted into hotels to accommodate guests from all over the world. A Courtyard generally has the beauty of classical oriental buildings, where guests can not only enjoy the traditional atmosphere but also learn more about the history of China.

Passage B

中华人民共和国国家旅游局(简称"国家旅游局")是国务院主管旅游工作的直属机构。国家旅游局的主要职能包括:统筹协调旅游业发展,制定发展政策、规划和标准;起草相关法律法规草案和规章并监督实施,指导地方旅游工作;制定国内旅游、入境旅游和出境旅游的市场开发战略并组织实施,组织国家旅游整体形象的对外宣传和重大推广活动;推动旅游国际交流与合作,承担与国际旅游组织合作的相关事务,制定出国旅游和边境旅游政策并组织实施,依法审批外国在我国境内设立的旅游机构,审查外商投资旅行社市场准入资格,依法审批经营国际旅游业务的旅行社,审批出国(境)旅游、边境旅游。

Case Study 案例分析

Hotel Industry Keeping ahead in Gwynedd

Keeping ahead of the competition and offering something different is the way to succeed according to two businesses in Dolgellau (威尔士多尔盖莱), Gwynedd (威尔士格温内思郡).

Ffynnon boutique hotel owners Steve Holt and Debra Harries researched the area before starting in business five years ago. Ms. Harries said their hard work paid off as they found no-one else was offering the same kind of "luxury" accommodation, and the business got a five star rating from day one.

This business employs five people, two full-time and three part-time. "We still do ongoing research, asking visitors how we can improve on what we do here," she said. "Service is important, maybe more important than the surroundings, and we have staff training and always take up suggestions of what people want, so that it's available the next time."

Geraint Roberts runs the Gwernan hotel in Dolgellau. He has invested heavily in a fishing lake that came with the property, upgrading access to include a path for the less able-bodied, along with new jetties. "It's a competitive world, and it's not enough just to offer somewhere to stay." he said.

The business employs six part-time staff in the summer, which decreases to week-end help over the winter, and despite the economic downturn the business had a "better than expected" summer.

High-quality-jobs within the sector are not the norm however, especially in more rural areas. "We would like to employ more to take the pressure off myself and my wife, but that isn't possible." "I was born in Aberdaron and whilst I was growing up there tourism was the mainstay of the local economy, as it is here. It has been important for years." he added.

Thinking:

1. What can you learn from the story? List at least 3 points.
2. "Service is important, maybe more important than the surroundings..." Do you agree with her? Why or why not?

Unit 5   Hotel Groups

▶▶ Lead-in 导读

　　当今世界有很多著名的酒店集团,如万豪、凯宾斯基、雅高、喜达屋等,它们都有着自己独特的企业文化、经营理念、发展历史和发展战略。本单元分别从亚洲、欧洲、美洲著名酒店集团中挑选三个最具代表性的酒店集团:亚洲最大的豪华酒店集团香格里拉、世界最大的酒店集团洲际和美国最大的酒店集团希尔顿,就其历史、发展、文化、规模和旗下品牌等方面进行介绍。

酒店英语阅读(上)

Reading 阅读

Text A

Shangri-La Hotel Group

Shangri-La Story

The Shangri-La story began in 1971 with its first deluxe hotel in Singapore. Inspired by the legendary land featured in James Hilton's 1933 novel, *Lost Horizon* ①, the name Shangri-La encapsulates the serenity and service for which its hotels and resorts are renowned worldwide.

Today, Hong Kong-based Shangri-La Hotels and Resorts is Asia Pacific's leading luxury hotel group

and is also regarded as one of the world's finest hotel ownership and management companies. With 72 hotels and resorts throughout Asia Pacific, North America, the Middle East, and Europe, the Shangri-La group has a room inventory of over 30,000. The "S" logo, which resembles uniquely Asian architectural forms, suggests majestic mountains reflected in the waters of a tranquil lake.②

Shangri-La Culture — Hospitality from the Heart

Through the years, Shangri-La's philosophy has been "Shangri-La Hospitality from a caring family"③. Shangri-La's commitment to providing guests with distinctive Asian standards of hospitality and service enables it to stand out amongst its peers. This quality remains the cornerstone of its reputation as a world-class hotel group. "Pride without arrogance" is of particular importance to Shangri-La. It takes pride in its achievements, while remaining outwardly humble.

Hotel Brands

- Shangri-La Hotels are five-star

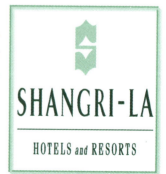

Vocabulary
encapsulate v. 压缩;概括
serenity n. 平静
majestic adj. 壮丽的
cornerstone n. 奠基石

Unit 5 Hotel Groups

luxury hotels located in premier city addresses across Asia and the Middle East, with future deluxe hotels underway in North America and Europe. "To treat a stranger as one of our own"④ characterizes the hospitality one can expect from Shangri-La.

engaging *adj.* 迷人的
complement *v.* 补充
buzz *v.* 东奔西走, 忙碌
exude *v.* 显示, 散发出
bestow *v.* 给予, 授予

● **Shangri-La Resorts** offer travelers and families a relaxing and engaging vacation in some of the world's most exotic destinations.

● **Traders Hotels**⑤ are a blend of thoughtful simplicity and the warmth and sincerity of Asian hospitality. Each Traders hotel is a vibrant, yet professional, place designed to complement guests at work, rest or play. Located in the business hubs of Asia and the Middle East, Traders Hotels are the practical choice for both business and leisure travelers.

● **Kerry Hotels** are vibrant places, buzzing with life and activity. Every Kerry hotel exudes a unique style and careful attentiveness that bestows a sense of individuality to all guests. Kerry Hotels is a new five-star brand in the Shangri-La family. It was launched in Shanghai and Beijing in 2011.

Notes

1. *Lost Horizon*: 英国作家詹姆斯·希尔顿1933年发表的传奇小说《消失的地平线》。该小说里面提到了香格里拉这个名字, 它所寓意的恬静、祥和、殷勤的服务, 完美地诠释了闻名遐迩的香格里拉酒店集团的精髓。
2. The "S" logo, which resembles uniquely Asian architectural forms, suggests majestic mountains reflected in the waters of a tranquil lake. 香格里拉的"S"标识借鉴了亚洲建筑的独特形式, 犹如雄伟壮丽的山脉倒映在宁静的湖面上。
3. Shangri-La's philosophy has been "Shangri-La Hospitality from a caring family". 香格里拉的经营理念是"香格里拉热情好客, 亲如家人"。
4. To treat a stranger as one of our own 宾至如归
5. Traders Hotels 盛贸饭店

InterContinental Hotel Group

InterContinental Story

The InterContinental Hotel Group (IHG) is a global hotel company whose goal is to create Great Hotels Guests Love①. It has more guest rooms than any other hotel company in the world — that's more than 678,000 rooms in over 4,600 hotels in nearly 100 countries and territories around the world. IHG operates hotels in three different ways — as a franchisor, a manager and on an owned and leased basis.

How We Behave

● **Do the right thing:** keep our promises and don't let people down; seek out the facts and trust our judgement; take responsibility and make decisions even when they're difficult.

● **Show we care:** treat people as individuals; look and listen for the little things that make a difference; use our experience to find new ways to deliver great service.

● **Aim higher:** put our hearts into learning new things; challenge and encourage ourselves and each other; always look for ways to improve.

● **Celebrate difference:** welcome different perspectives and listen to everyone's ideas; be respectful of all cultures and look to learn from others; play an active role in the communities in which we operate.

● **Work better together:** work hard to develop excellent working relationships with colleagues; think about what we do and how it might affect others; trust and support each other.

Hotel Brands

● **InterContinental Hotels & Resorts** is the most prestigious brand of the IHG group, located in major cities in over 60 countries worldwide, offering business and leisure travelers the highest level

Vocabulary

franchisor *n.* 特许经营者

of service and facilities.

- **Crowne Plaza** offers premium accommodation, designed for the discerning business and leisure traveler who appreciates simplified elegance.

premium *adj.* 高级的
discerning *adj.* 有眼光的
style-conscious *adj.* 时尚的
multiple *adj.* 多个的

- **Indigo Hotels**② are located in urban, mid-town and suburban areas, close to businesses, restaurants and entertainment venues, and designed for the style-conscious traveler.

- **Holiday Inn** offers today's business and leisure travelers dependability, friendly service, modern facilities and excellent value.

- **Holiday Inn Express**③ (or Express by Holiday Inn) is a fresh, clean simple hotel choice offering comfort, convenience and good value.

- **Staybridge Suites**④ is an all-suite hotel brand for extended stay guests looking for a residential-style hotel for business, relocation or leisure.

- **Candlewood Suites**' high-quality accommodation caters to mid-market business and leisure travelers looking for a multiple night hotel stay.

- **EVEN™ Hotels** is the first hotel brand designed for business and leisure travelers who maintain a healthy and active lifestyle.

- **HUALUX Hotels & Resorts**⑤, an upscale brand, designed specially for Chinese travelers.

Notes

1. Great Hotels Guests Love 客人挚爱的杰出酒店。洲际酒店集团(IHG)是一家以"客人挚爱的杰出酒店"(Great Hotels Guests Love) 为核心目标的国际酒店管理集团。
2. Indigo Hotels 英迪格酒店。现已遍布全球众多主要城市,以清新的设计、个性化的服务和融合本地风情的独有特色,为宾客提供无尽的灵感和愉悦的住宿体验。
3. Holiday Inn Express 智选假日酒店
4. Staybridge Suites 品牌是一个别具一格的饭店概念,专为满足那些来自世界各地需连续入住饭店五晚或以上的旅客的需求。酒店设有无间隔、一间或两间睡房的套房,套房设施包括双人床或特大单人床、沙发床,互动电视,面积宽敞及光线充足的工作室,备有煮食用具及家用电冰箱、微波炉的厨房,以及其他具有家居特色的设备。
5. HUALUX Hotels & Resorts 华邑酒店及度假村

Hilton Hotel Group

Hilton Story

Conrad N. Hilton[①] began with a 40-room hotel in a small Texas town in 1919. Today, Hilton Worldwide is the world's preeminent hospitality company, stretching across 24 time zones. Hilton hotels are located in world capitals, rural roadsides, trade centers, vacation destinations, and everywhere in between. When Conrad N. Hilton opened the first hotel to bear the Hilton name in 1925, he aimed to operate the best hotel in Texas. As a result of his commitment, leadership, and innovation, today Hilton is one of the most respected brands in the world.

Hilton Values

- Hospitality: we're passionate about delivering exceptional guest experiences.
- Integrity: we do the right thing, all the time.
- Leadership: we're leaders in our industry and in our communities.
- Teamwork: we're team players in everything we do.
- Ownership: we're the owners of our actions and decisions.
- Now: we operate with a sense of urgency and discipline.

Hotel Brands

- **Waldorf Astoria Hotels & Resorts** reflect the culture and history of their extraordinary locations, as well as fresh, modern expressions of Waldorf Astoria's rich legacy.
- **Conrad Hotels & Resorts** offers guests a one-of-a-kind experience and service. It's the destination of a new generation of global travelers for whom life, business, and pleasure seamlessly intersect.
- **Hilton Hotels & Resorts,** one of the most recognized names in the industry, offers travelers a world of authentic experiences. The brand continues to be the innovative, forward-thinking global leader of hospitality.
- **DoubleTree by Hilton™** all starts with a warm chocolate chip cookie, a simple touch that sets the tone to create a rewarding

Vocabulary

preeminent *adj.* 卓越超群的
one-of-a-kind *adj.* 独一无二的
seamlessly *adv.* 无缝地
forward-thinking *adj.* 有远见的

experience for a guest's entire stay.② It understands that doing the little things well can mean everything.

- **Hilton Garden Inn**™ is the award-winning, upscale, yet affordable, hotel brand.

- **Embassy Suites** leads the category in the all suite, full-service, upscale hotel experience. Whether you're traveling for business or leisure, best-in-class customer service is provided here.

- **Hampton**③ provides incredible value, friendly service, free breakfast and Internet, Clean and Fresh Hampton Beds, and well-appointed rooms.

- **Homewood Suites by Hilton**™④ sets the standard in upscale, extended stay, offering home-like comforts and quality bundled services.

- **Home2 Suites by Hilton**⑤ is creating a more forward-thinking extended-stay experience by delivering unexpected style, enhanced flexibility, expanded spaces, and differentiated amenities.

- **Hilton Grand Vacations** offers a passport to endless vacation memories for those aspiring to the good life.

best-in-class *adj.* 一流的
well-appointed *adj.* 设备齐全的
bundled *adj.* 捆绑的

Notes

1. Conrad N. Hilton 希尔顿（1887—1979），美国旅馆业巨头，人称旅店帝王，在1919年创建第一家"希尔顿酒店"。希尔顿经营旅馆业的座右铭是："你今天对客人微笑了吗？"这也是他所著的《宾至如归》(*Be My Guest*) 一书的核心内容。

2. DoubleTree by Hilton™ all starts with a warm chocolate chip cookie, a simple touch that sets the tone to create a rewarding experience for a guest's entire stay. 希尔顿逸林酒店及度假村的贴心服务从送上热巧克力香脆曲奇开始，小小的心意为宾客在整个住宿期间将会享有的满足体验定下基调。

3. Hampton 希尔顿欢朋酒店是一个屡获殊荣的酒店品牌，主要服务于注重价值及讲究品质的旅客。宾客可在此享受到高品质的住宿、具有竞争力的房价以及热情友好的服务。

4. Homewood Suites by Hilton™ 希尔顿欣庭酒店是全套房住宅风格酒店，主要服务于追求居家体验的旅客。

5. Home2 Suites by Hilton 希尔顿惠庭酒店是彰显创新精神的中档长期住宿型酒店。

酒店英语阅读（上）

Useful Words and Expressions 实用词汇与表达

1. stand out 脱颖而出
2. take pride in 以……为自豪
3. seek out 找出
4. take decisions 做出抉择
5. feature in 在……中起重要作用，做主要角色
6. bear the...name 以……命名
7. with a sense of... 具有……感
8. set the tone to 定下基调
9. set the standard (in) 设置标准
10. aspire to 渴望

Practical Reading 实用文体欣赏

Lunch & Dinner Menu

Appetizers & Salads

Sashimi & Sushi with Condiments & Miso Soup	RMB 90
Caesar Salad with Iceberg Lettuce, Croutons, Candied Bacon, Parmesan & Caesar Dressing	RMB 50
Extras Served with Your Caesar Salad:	
Grilled Chicken	RMB 10
Smoked Salmon	RMB 20

From The Soup Kettle

Chef's Seasonal Soup	RMB 40
Hearty Goulash Soup	RMB 38

Asian Main Delights

Udon or Soba Noodle With Egg or Deep Fried Bean Curd	RMB 70

From The Grill

Imported Rib Eye Steak (230gr)	RMB 250
Grilled King Prawns (Per 100gr)	RMB 200
Yours Choice Of Sauce: Black Pepper, Garlic	

Just Dessert

Macadamia Cheese Cake	RMB 40
Fruit Platter with Yoghurt	RMB 40

Unit 5 Hotel Groups

Knowledge 趣味小知识

西式早餐

西式早餐主要供应一些选料精细、粗纤维少、营养丰富的食品,如各种蛋类、饭料、面包等。西式早餐一般可分为两种:一种是美式早餐(American Breakfast),英国、美国、加拿大、澳大利亚及新西兰等以英语为母语的国家的早餐都属于此类;另一种是欧陆式(Continental Breakfast),德国、法国等地的早餐属于此类。美式早餐品种丰富,比较流行,主要供应各种蛋类,再配以火腿、咸肉等,以及各种谷类食品(如面包、麦片、玉米片等)和饮料(如果汁、咖啡、红茶、牛奶等)。欧陆式早餐比较简单,属于清淡式早餐,不包括蛋类和肉类,主要供应各种面包(如牛角包、吐司等),再配以黄油、果酱或蜂蜜等,以及各种饮料(如果汁、咖啡、红茶、牛奶、热巧克力等)。以上两种通常以套餐形式提供,客人也可以享用零点早餐(A La Carte Breakfast),其不同之处在于:零点早餐是供客人单点的早餐,每项食品单独定价;并且可以选择蛋类和肉类的制作方法。

敬酒礼仪

敬酒分为正式敬酒和普通敬酒。正式敬酒是指在宴会开始时,由主人向大家集体敬酒,并同时说祝酒词。普通敬酒是在主人正式敬酒之后,各个来宾和主人之间或者来宾之间互相敬酒。

当主人向集体敬酒、说祝酒词时,所有人应停止用餐或喝酒。主人提议干杯时,所有人要端起酒杯站起来,互相碰杯或示意。国际通行做法是,敬酒不一定要喝干,但至少举杯轻抿,以示对主人的尊重。无论是主人或是来宾,在座位上向集体敬酒时,首先要站起身来,面带微笑,手拿酒杯,面朝大家。敬酒一般情况下应以年龄大小、职位高低、宾主身份为序,在敬酒前需考虑好敬酒的顺序,主次分明,避免出现尴尬情况。

中餐中不仅敬酒,而且劝酒较多,时常要求干杯,而西餐中只敬酒不劝酒,且敬酒不必真正碰杯。

Exercises 练习

1. Phrase Translation

1) 客房量
2) 时区
3) 商务和休闲旅客
4) 迎合
5) 脱颖而出
6) set the tone to
7) take pride in
8) extended stay guests
9) take decisions
10) business hub

2. Passage Translation

Passage A

Kempinski aims to be renowned as hoteliers who offer luxurious hospitality in the grand European style. We serve the kind of people who expect excellence and value individuality. The strategy guiding us throughout is long-term and focused on our enterprise value. Every aspect of Kempinski is geared towards serving guests who expect excellence and value individuality. The fact that Kempinski is not publicly listed, but rather a private company, plus the support we enjoy from our shareholders, means we can focus on a long-term strategy, creating value that is sustainable. We believe that the Kempinski brand promise of luxury hospitality provided with European flair can be best delivered through a decentralised approach. Our trust in and empowerment of staff in our regional offices means we can deliver our brand promise coherently, while respecting the cultures specific to each region, country and property.

Passage B

凯悦是一家世界知名的酒店集团,在业内负有盛名。在50多年的发展历史中,始终贯彻以客为先的服务精神。我们的使命是提供真诚的款待,为每天接触的客人带来宾至如归的美妙感受。我们专注于达成使命,并务求每一环节尽善尽美,使员工、宾客和顾客都以优越的品牌引以为荣。我们坚持一系列代表凯悦文化的核心价值观,并矢志追求其使命和目标。

 Case Study 案例分析

John Willard Marriott

John Willard Marriott was born on September 17, 1900, the second of eight children of Hyrum Willard Marriott and Ellen Morris Marriott. As a youngster, he quickly learned to rely on his own judgment and initiative. "My father gave me the responsibility of a man," said Marriott many years later. "He would tell me what he wanted done, but never said much about how to do it. It was up to me to find out for myself." He dreamed of a life beyond the family farm. After completing a two-year mission for the Mormon Church in New England, Marriott returned to Utah in 1921 to pursue a college degree, graduating first from Weber Junior College and then the University of Utah. Tuition money came from assorted jobs.

While finishing up at the university, Marriott hatched plans for starting a business of his own. He had passed through hot, muggy Washington, D.C., at the end of his mission and recognized a tailor-made market for A&W Root Beer. He secured the A&W franchise for Washington, D.C. and headed east in the spring of 1927. Marriott and partner Hugh Colton pooled $6,000 to buy equipment and rent space for their tiny operation. On May 20, 1927, the duo opened their nine-stool root beer stand at 3128 14th Street, NW.

For the next 58 years, J. Willard Marriott rarely rested. Even when his older son took over most major responsibilities after being named the company's CEO in 1972, the founder could not bring himself to retire. "Take care of your employees and they'll take care of your customers," he constantly advised Marriott's managers, voicing a deeply held belief that remains the keystone of the company's culture.

Willard Marriott summed up the personal philosophy that drove him his entire life: "A man should keep on being constructive, and do constructive things. He should take part in the things that go on in this wonderful world. He should be someone to be reckoned with. He should live life and make every day count, to the very end. Sometimes it's tough. But that's what I'm going to do."

Thinking:

1. What can you learn from the story? List at least 3 points.
2. What philosophy drove J. Willard Marriott his entire life? What do you think of it and what is your philosophy of life?

Unit 6　Schools and Education

▶▶ Lead-in 导读

世界上有很多著名的酒店管理学院,它们凭借自己独特的校园文化和教育理念,为酒店行业培养和输送了无数的杰出人才。本单元将选取被称为世界三大酒店管理名校的美国康奈尔大学、瑞士洛桑酒店管理学院和格里昂酒店管理学院,就其发展历史、校园文化、优势特色等方面进行介绍。

Unit 6 Schools and Education

Reading 阅读

Text A

Cornell University-School of Hotel Administration

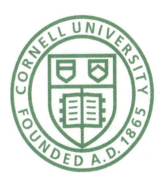

Hospitality Leadership Through Learning

Founded in 1922, Cornell University's School of Hotel Administration① was the first collegiate program in hospitality management. Today it is regarded as the world leader in its field.

The school's highly talented and motivated students learn from 60 full-time faculty members, all experts in their chosen disciplines, and all dedicated to teaching, research and service. Learning takes place in state-of-the-art classrooms, in the on-campus Statler hotel②, and in varied industry settings around the world. The result: a supremely accomplished alumni group - corporate executives and entrepreneurs who advance the industry and share their wisdom and experience with our students and faculty.

History

"Life is service—the one who progresses is the one who gives his fellow men a little more — a little better service."—E. M. Statler③

Founded in 1922 at the request of leading hotel magnates and the American Hotel Association, the Cornell School of Hotel Administration has a rich history. The founders wanted to create a first-rate academic institution providing a field of study for the "science" of running hotels and restaurants.

The Cornell Hotel School, the world's first undergraduate hospitality management degree program, began with 21 students under the direction of a single professor, Howard B. Meek. Cornell was the ideal Ivy League school④ to initiate this endeavor, since the university's original mission in 1865 was to "found an institution where any person

---

Vocabulary

collegiate *adj.* 大学的；学院的
discipline *n.* 学科
state-of-the-art *adj.* 最先进的
setting *n.* 环境
alumni *n.* (男)校友
advance *vt.* 推动某事发展
magnate *n.* 富豪，权贵；巨头
ivy *adj.* 常春藤联盟的
mission *n.* 代表团；使命

can find instruction in any study."

The Statler Hotel

The Statler Hotel is the showcase for Cornell's world-renowned School of Hotel Administration, and, for many visitors, the gateway to the university as a whole. The Statler Hotel hosts campus visitors, visiting scholars, prospective and current students and their families, and alumni. With its elegant banquet rooms and state-of-the-art conference facilities, the hotel serves as the venue for many important campus events and meetings.

showcase *n.* 显示优点的东西
gateway *n.* 门；入口；途径
venue *n.* 会场

As a "Teaching Hotel," ⑤ it also integrates several courses into hotel operations and provides career-related job experience for students. It serves not only the school's undergraduate and graduate students, but also industry professionals from around the world who use The Statler Hotel while taking advanced hospitality service and management courses through the school's Office of Executive Education.

Notes

1. 康奈尔大学、洛桑酒店管理学院和格里昂酒店管理学院被称为世界三大酒店管理名校。
2. Statler hotel 斯塔特勒饭店。1908年1月，美国的斯塔特勒(Ellsworth. M. Statler)在巴伏劳(Buffalo)开设了斯塔特勒饭店(Statler Hotel)，从而开创了饭店发展的新纪元。
3. E. M. Statler 斯塔特勒是美国，也是世界饭店业的开山祖师之一。现代饭店业中的许多服务及广告促销等做法都是从他这里开始的。他对于培训特别重视，著名的康奈尔大学饭店管理系中有一幢他投资兴建的教学楼。
4. Ivy League school 常春藤盟校或常春藤联盟。Ivy League 成立于1954年，是由美国东北部地区的8所大学组成的体育赛事联盟。这8所学校都是美国名校，也是美国生产最多罗德奖学金得主的大学联盟。常春藤盟校包括：布朗大学、哥伦比亚大学、康奈尔大学、达特茅斯学院、哈佛大学、宾夕法尼亚大学、普林斯顿大学、耶鲁大学。所有的常春藤盟校都是私立大学，和公立大学一样，它们同时接受联邦政府资助和私人捐赠，用于学术研究。
5. Teaching Hotel 教学酒店

Text B

Lausanne Hotel School—EHL

The Lausanne Hotel School (French: École hôtelière de Lausanne, EHL) is a Swiss hospitality school, located in Lausanne①.

Founded in 1893, EHL was the world's first trade-school to focus on hospitality education. Since the late 20th century, it began to offer university-level degrees.

In Switzerland, the school is the only institute of hospitality management offering advanced programmes which are recognized by the Swiss government. It is part of the University of Applied Sciences Western Switzerland. It is also accredited as an Institution of Higher Education by the New England Association of Schools and Colleges (NEASC) in the United States and the Bologna Process② in Europe.

History

Ecole hôtelière de Lausanne was founded over a hundred years ago, in 1893, during the Belle Epoque③ when Switzerland was experiencing an unprecedented boom in tourism and there was an urgent need for skilled and professional personnel, at every level from management on down.

This was the era of the grand palaces and magnificent hotels — still visible today — built along the shore of Geneva④ and in mountain resorts high above the lake, in order to accommodate a growing international, and often wealthy and famous, clientele. The school was founded in response to this need. At the time, the idea of a hotel school was revolutionary. Its founder, Jacques Tschumi, an influential member of the Swiss Hotel Association, had to persuade his rather reticent fellow members that the project was a realistic and viable one. His vision was soon to be proven well-founded.

A Campus — and also a Hotel

The Ecole hôtelière de Lausanne is run like a hotel, with rooms and accommodation, reception, conference facilities, and five

Vocabulary

trade-school n. 中专，职业学校
accredit vt. 委托，授权
Bologna n. 博洛尼亚（意大利城市）
revolutionary adj. 创新的
reticent adj. 含蓄的；谨慎的
viable adj. 可实施的

different restaurants including a fine-dining restaurant open to the public, four main kitchens and four satellite kitchens, a state-of-the-art auditorium and banqueting facilities. Throughout the students' studies, they will be experiencing a hospitality enterprise from the inside. At the beginning, their experience will be alternately as host and client, working behind the scenes and then enjoying their experience as a guest. Later, they will be supervising others and using the school as a laboratory to develop concepts and events.

Notes

1. Lausanne 洛桑。瑞士西部城市,位于日内瓦湖北岸。
2. New England Association of Schools and Colleges 新英格兰学校学院协会。这是一个区域教育认证机构。该机构负责审核高等教育及职业资格。
   Bologna Process:博洛尼亚进程。博洛尼亚进程是欧洲诸国间在高等教育领域互相衔接的一个项目,以确保各国高等教育标准相当。体系得名于1999年欧洲29个国家在意大利的博洛尼亚大学签订的《博洛尼亚宣言》。随后,该体系对所有愿意参加的欧洲国家开放。
3. Belle Epoque 美好年代。美好年代(法语:Belle Époque)是欧洲社会史上的一段时期,从19世纪末开始至第一次世界大战爆发而结束。美好年代是后人对这一时代的回顾,这个时期被上流阶级认为是一个"黄金时代",此时的欧洲处于一个相对和平的时期,随着资本主义及工业革命的发展,科学技术日新月异,欧洲的文化、艺术及生活方式等都在这个时期发展得日臻成熟。此时期约与英国的维多利亚时代后期及爱德华时代相互重叠。
4. Geneva 日内瓦城。位于瑞士西南部。

Text C

Glion Institute of Higher Education

Hospitality Management School

Glion Institute of Higher Education is an international hospitality management institution in Switzerland. Opened in the fall of 1962 in the former Bellevue Hotel①, Glion Hotel School (as it was then named) was the first private, university-level Swiss hotel management school. As a

Unit 6 Schools and Education

private, for-profit institution, GIHE has built its reputation for excellence and has become a leader in hospitality education worldwide.

More than a simple hotel school, Glion Institute of Higher Education is accredited by the New England Association of Schools and Colleges (NEASC)② to deliver programs leading to diploma, associate's③, bachelor's, postgraduate and master's level qualifications in international hospitality management, and event, sport and entertainment management.

Vision

Through its challenging academic programs, structured living environment, craft-based learning, and the "Glion Spirit"④, the Glion Institute of Higher Education develops innovative leaders for a broad array of service industries.

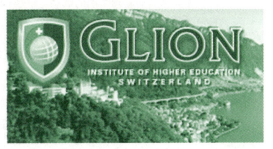

Mission

The Glion Institute of Higher Education offers management-focused programs for the hospitality and other service industries. All programs emphasize the development of generic thinking skills, the understanding of contemporary management theory, and the integration of theory and practice. The "Glion Spirit" and GIHE's academic programs prepare individuals for rapid progress to international managerial positions.

The values that guide GIHE toward their vision are

- To provide educational breadth coupled with optional specializations;
- To develop leadership, enterprise and entrepreneurial skills;
- To respect differences of culture;
- To act with integrity;
- To foster an international perspective;
- To guide students to increasing responsibility.

Global Opportunities

Today, Glion is extending its transformative education to a new

Vocabulary

for-profit adj. 以盈利为目的的
diploma n. 学位证书，毕业文凭
generic adj. 一般的
managerial adj. 经理的；管理上的
breadth n. (知识、兴趣等的)广泛
specialization n. 特别化；专门化
transformative adj. 有改革能力的

campus in London⑤, Europe's business hub. On global campuses, Glion is offering an international experience to prepare students for top positions in fast-growing global hospitality, tourism and service industries worldwide.

Notes

1. Bellevue Hotel 贝尔维尤酒店
2. New England Association of Schools and Colleges (NEASC) 新英格兰学校学院协会。这是一个区域教育认证机构。该机构负责审核高等教育及职业资格。
3. associate's degree 准学士学位,专科毕业证书
4. craft-based learning 基于实践的教学。Glion Spirit：格里昂精神。在过去的40年里,来自世界各地的毕业生都曾领略了"格里昂魅力",学到了著名的"格里昂精神(Glion Spirit)"。这两个独一无二的特征是格里昂酒店管理学院的驱动力,也给了格里昂酒店管理学院所有毕业生成功开创专业人生的自信和激情。
5. 格里昂伦敦校区位于风景如画的罗汉普顿大学英国校区内,距离伦敦市中心很近。格里昂伦敦新校区为学生提供了独特的学习环境:在欧洲的商业中心伦敦接受世界顶级酒店管理院校的教育。

Useful Words and Expressions 实用词汇与表达

1. be regarded as 被认为;被认为是
2. at the request of 应……之请求,鉴于……之请求
3. integrate...into... 使成一体
4. in response to 对……做出反应;响应
5. be surrounded by 被……包围
6. open to the public 向公众开放
7. more than 不只是
8. act with integrity 行事正直
9. foster an ... perspective 培养具有……视野的人才
10. extend...to... (使)达到,伸展到;扩大到

Practical Reading 实用文体欣赏

Apology Card

Dear Mr. Tsai,

May I first of all thank you for staying with us.

I sincerely apologize for the inconvenience caused by the problem of air conditioner last night, and it had been fixed by our engineer this morning.

According to ABC Behaviors, we would like to arrange some amenities with our compliments.

Your patience & understanding is greatly appreciated.

Please contact Guest Relations Manager at extension-0 should you inquire any further assistance.

Sincerely,

Zoe Zhong

Guest Relations Manager

Knowledge 趣味小知识

西餐服务形式

西餐服务经过多年的发展,在各国和各地区都形成了自己的特色。常见的西餐服务形式有:法式服务、俄式服务、美式服务、英式服务、综合式服务及自助式服务。

法式服务:是指服务员采用手推车或旁桌现场为顾客加热和调味菜肴及切割菜肴等服务。它注重服务程序和礼节礼貌,需要较多人力,用餐费用

较高。

俄式服务：是指将装有整齐和美观菜肴的大浅盘端给所有顾客过目并分菜。每一个餐桌只需要一个服务员，方式简单快速，服务时不需要较大的空间。

美式服务：比较简单快捷。一名服务员可以照看数张餐台，餐具和人工成本都比较低。

英式服务：又称家庭式服务，是指服务员从厨房将烹制好的菜肴传送到餐厅，由顾客中的主人亲自动手切肉装盘，并配上蔬菜，服务员把装盘的菜肴依次端送给每一位客人。

综合式服务：是一种融合了法式服务、俄式服务和美式服务的综合服务方式。

自助式服务：是指把事先准备好的菜肴摆在餐台上，客人自己动手选择菜点，然后拿到餐桌上用餐。服务员的工作主要是餐前布置，餐中撤掉用过的餐具和酒杯，补充餐台上的菜肴等。

西餐的席位排列

西餐的席位排列与中餐有一定区别，中餐多为圆桌，而西餐多使用长桌。西餐的席位排列原则如下：

女士优先 在西餐礼仪里，往往体现女士优先的原则。排定用餐席位时，一般女主人为第一主人，在主位就位。而男主人为第二主人，坐在第二主人的位置上。

距离定位 西餐桌上席位的尊卑，由距离主位的远近而定。距主位近的位置要高于距主位远的位置。

以右为尊 就某一具体位置而言，按礼仪规范其右侧要高于左侧之位。在西餐排位时，男主宾要排在女主人的右侧，女主宾排在男主人的右侧，按此原则，依次排列。

面门为上 按礼仪要求，面对餐厅正门的位子要高于背对餐厅正门的位子。

交叉排列 男女交叉排列，熟人和生人也交叉排列。在西方人看来，宴会场合是要拓展人际关系，这样交叉排列，用意就是让人们能多和周围客人聊天认识，达到社交目的。

Unit 6 Schools and Education

Exercises 练习

1. Phrase Translation

1）连锁酒店
2）客房入住率
3）房价
4）礼宾服务
5）送餐服务
6) half board
7) walk-in guests
8) adjoining room
9) light refreshments
10) dust off

2. Passage Translation

Passage A

Since the establishment of its first hotel school in 1982, SEG has grown to become the world's leading hospitality education network. SEG's outstanding success has set new standards in the hospitality industry and provides inspiration to its graduates. SEG member schools are 100% Swiss owned ensuring students receive a quality education with a distinctive Swiss style that is renowned worldwide. SEG stands for a truly international education provider: there are over 80 nationalities represented on SEG campuses; practically oriented education combined with a strong academic focus, developed specifically to meet industry needs. SEG Hotel Management Schools in Switzerland are: César Ritz Hospitality College Switzerland, Culinary Institute Switzerland, Hotel Institute Montreux HIM, International School of Hotel Management IHTTI, and Swiss Hotel Management School SHMS.

Passage B
欢迎辞

尊敬的宾客：

欢迎您下榻ABC酒店！

对于您的到来，我们酒店全体员工都感到非常荣幸，此《服务指南》为您详细介绍了酒店的各项服务及设施。若您有什么需要，请直接与酒店各部门联系，我们将竭诚为您效劳。

在ABC酒店，您是我们的第一关注，我们将为您提供尽善尽美的服务。如果您对我们的服务及设施有什么意见或建议，请及时联系我们，或者填写摆放于客房桌子上的"宾客意见表"。

酒店英语阅读（上）

最后，希望您在这里一切愉快，并期待您的再次光临，谢谢！

ABC 酒店
总经理

Case Study 案例分析

Conrad Hilton

Conrad Nicholson Hilton (December 25, 1887-January 3, 1979) was an American hotelier. He is well known for being the founder of the Hilton Hotels chain.

The most enduring influence to shape Hilton's philanthropic philosophy beyond that of his parents was the Roman Catholic Church and his sisters. He credited his mother with guiding him to prayer and the church whenever he was troubled or dismayed — from the boyhood loss of a beloved pony to severe financial losses during the Great Depression.

As a young boy, Hilton developed entrepreneurial skills working at his father's general store in Socorro County, New Mexico. This was followed by varied experiences, including a stint as a representative in New Mexico's first State Legislature and a career decision to become a banker.

It was with the intention of buying a bank that he arrived in Texas at the height of the oil boom. He bought his first hotel instead, the 40-room Mobley Hotel in Cisco, Texas, in 1919, when a bank purchase fell through. The hotel did such brisk business that rooms changed hands as much as three times a day, and the dining room was converted into additional rooms to meet the demand.

He went on to buy and build hotels throughout Texas, including the high rise Dallas Hilton, opened in 1925; the Abilene Hilton in 1927; Waco Hilton in 1928; and El Paso Hilton in 1930. He built his first hotel outside of Texas in 1939 in Albuquerque, New Mexico, today known as the Hotel Andaluz. When Conrad N. Hilton opened the first hotel to bear the Hilton name in 1925, he aimed to operate the best hotel in Texas. As a result of his commitment, leadership, and innovation, today Hilton is one of the most respected brands in the world.

During the Great Depression Hilton was nearly forced into bankruptcy and lost several of his hotels. Nonetheless he was retained as manager of a combined chain, and eventually regained control of his remaining eight hotels.

During the 1950s and 1960s, Hilton Hotels' worldwide expansion facilitated both American tourism and overseas business by American corporations. It was the world's first international hotel chain, at the same time promulgating a certain worldwide standard for hotel accommodations. In all, Hilton eventually owned 188 hotels in thirty-eight cities in the U.S.

Hilton received honorary degrees from the University of Detroit (1953), DePaul University (1954), Barat College (1955), Adelphi College (1957), Sophia University, Tokyo (1963), and the University of Albuquerque (1975). Hilton's autobiography, Be My Guest, was published in 1957 by Prentice Hall. In 1966, Hilton was succeeded as president by his son Barron and was elected chairman of the board.

Thinking:
1. What was the most enduring influence to shape Hilton's philanthropic philosophy beyond that of his parents?
2. What qualities are necessary to become famous?

Unit 7　Etiquette and Service

▶▶ Lead-in 导读

如其他行业一样,当今社会酒店业的竞争也越来越激烈。酒店要想在竞争中保持有利地位,良好的服务与礼仪必不可少。实际上,服务与礼仪始终贯穿于酒店的方方面面。良好的服务与礼仪对改善员工服务形象、提升员工服务水平至关重要,同时也会为酒店赢得良好的经济效益和社会效益。

Unit 7 Etiquette and Service

Reading 阅 读

Text A

Proper Serving Etiquette

Proper serving etiquette is a list of rules about how food should be presented and served at formal restaurants. The proper etiquette of a restaurant's wait staff is very crucial in providing the guests an outstanding dining experience. Here is a list of proper wait staff etiquette in serving guests.

Physical Appearance[①]

Be neat and clean. Chef coats should be clean and worn suitably. Long hair must be tied and combed. Stand up straight, do not slouch.

Behavior

Wit and charm combined with courtesy and professionalism are the ingredients needed in this occupation. When there's a need to talk to each other, keep the voice low.

Moving About

When moving through a crowded restaurant, walk smoothly and slowly. When compelled to get someone's attention in order to pass, touch the elbow so as not to offend the guest.

Taking Orders

When people are served, the tradition is to start with the guest of honor,[②] followed by the women in the party, the men, the hostess, and finally the host. If the delineations between guests are not clear, servers start with the oldest woman at the table, and work their way down to the youngest man.

Serving of Plates

Plates should be served and cleared all at once[③]. The courses should be served simultaneously too, to allow the guests to start their meal at the same time. Utensils ought to be different in between courses.

Vocabulary

slouch v. 无精打采地站
courtesy n. 礼貌
delineation n. 描述,圈定
simultaneously adv. 同时
utensil n. 用具,器皿

酒店英语阅读（上）

Serving the Food and Drinks

Food and drinks are customarily served from the left side of the guest.④ Wines are served from the right side. Always use a tray in serving drinks. Stemmed glasses should be held at the stem.

Waiting on the Guests

Always be on the lookout for guests who might need anything else. Make sure that the table has water and everyone's table needs are attended to.

Clearing of the Plates

Clearing of the plates should be done after everyone has eaten, making sure that the guests will not feel rushed as you do so.

Bringing the Bill

The bill should only be brought out if someone asks for it. Do not get the signed bill or the payment unless the guest says so.

Precise etiquette in serving guests varies, as this is reliant on cultural norms and restaurant rules.⑤ Each region, and each restaurant has its own rules to follow. But knowing and mastering the above general rules can really be helpful in developing serving skills.

Notes

1. physical appearance 仪容仪表
2. guest of honor 贵宾
3. Plates should be served and cleared all at once. 应同时上菜，同时撤盘。
4. Food and drinks are customarily served from the left side of the guest. 按照惯例，应从客人的左边为客人提供菜品和酒饮。
5. Precise etiquette in serving guests varies, as this is reliant on cultural norms and restaurant rules. 文化标准和餐厅制度不同，宾客服务礼仪的要求也会有所不同。

Text B

Chinese Table Manners

A multitude of etiquette considerations occur when dining in China. There are some special differences from manners in western

Vocabulary

considerations *n.* 注意事项

countries.

Seating

A round dining table is more popular than a rectangular or square one. The guest of honor is always seated to the right of the host; the next in line① will sit on his left. Guests should be seated after the host's invitation, and it is discourteous to seat guests at the place where the dishes are served. Dining may only begin once the host and all his guests are seated.

Using

On a typical Chinese dining table there are always cups, bowls, small dishes, chopsticks and spoons. Dishes are always presented in the center of the table. The Chinese are particular about the use of chopsticks. There are many no-no's② such as twiddling with chopsticks, licking chopsticks, or using them to stir up the food, gesture with them or point them at others. Never stick chopsticks in the center of rice, as this is the way to sacrifice and is therefore considered to be inauspicious.

Serving

A formal dining is always accompanied by tea, beer or white spirit. The one who sits closest to the teapot, or wine bottle, should pour them for others from the senior and superior to the junior and inferior. And when other people fill your cup or glass, you should express your thanks.

Toasting

A toast to others is a characteristic of Chinese dining.③ When all people are seated and all cups are filled, the host should toast others first, together with some simple prologue to let the dining start. During the dining after the senior's toast, you can toast anyone from superior to inferior at their convenience. When someone toasts you, you should immediately stop eating and drinking to accept and toast in response. If you are far from someone you want to toast, then you can use your cup or glass to rap on the table to attract attention rather than raise your voice.④

Conventionally, if you are invited to a formal banquet, all the dishes should not be eaten up completely, or you will give the host the impression that he has not provided a good banquet and the food was insufficient. After dining, guests should leave once the host has left the table.

---

rectangular *n.* 长方形
discourteous *adj.* 失礼的
twiddle *n.* 旋转，摆弄
lick *v.* 舔
inauspicious *adj.* 不祥的
inferior *n.* 下级
prologue *n.* 开场白
rap *v.* 敲击,碰
conventionally *adv.* 照惯例
insufficient *adj.* 不足的

Notes

1. next in line 下一个，下一位
2. no-no's 同 no-nos，为 no-no 的复数形式，意为禁忌。
3. A toast to others is a characteristic Chinese dining. 敬酒是中式餐桌礼仪的一大特色。
4. If you are far from someone you want to toast, then you can use your cup or glass to rap on the table to attract attention rather than raise your voice. 倘若你想敬酒的人座位离你较远，你可以用酒杯碰击一下桌子来吸引对方的注意，不要大声喊叫。

Text C

Keys to Delivering Good Service

Everyone understands that customers want superior service and that better service leads to better profits.① Understanding it is one thing; doing it is another. Here are five things that any organization that cares about good service can do.

Don't forget who you are.

Companies that succeed create a service strategy for each market segment and stick to it. They make certain that everyone who works for them understands what they are selling and who they want to sell it to.

Encourage every employee to act like a manager.

Managers understand the need for repeat business②; employees may not. Service-oriented companies motivate, train and empower their employees to act like the company they work for is their own business.

Handle moments of truth correctly.

Service-oriented businesses concentrate their efforts on making sure that moments of truth③ are handled correctly. For hotels, an important moment of truth occurs when guests check in or out and come face-to-face with a hotel employee. Although there are certain check-in/check-out routines that must be followed, guests should be given individual attention so they feel their needs are being addressed in a personal way.

Hire good people and keep them happy.

Turnover is the worst enemy superior service has. Superior

Vocabulary

motivate v. 激励
empower v. 授权，使能够
turnover n. 人员流动

Unit 7 Etiquette and Service

companies make every effort to recruit, hire and hold onto people who have the right personalities. Many companies today hire for attitude rather than skill④. Skills that are learned on the job are often more easily upgraded than attitudes that employees bring with them.

Respond in a timely manner.

Waiting, for guests, is a hallmark of poor service. At family restaurants, most guests expect their food to be on the table in 30 minutes or less. No one likes to be put on hold when making a reservation. Excellent companies are constantly monitoring the waiting time for their guests and looking for ways to decrease it, or at least make it less stressful.

Every organization and every situation is unique. Managers need to develop their own lists of key service criteria and ways to implement them. It's the difference between winning and losing the battle for satisfied customers.

recruit *v.* 招聘
hallmark *n.* 特点,标志

Notes

1. Everyone understands that customers want superior service and the better service leads to better profits. 众所周知,顾客期待优质服务;服务越好,效益越高。
2. repeat business 回头生意
3. moments of truth 关键时刻,缩写为MOT。上世纪80年代,北欧航空卡尔森总裁提出:平均每位顾客在接受其公司服务的过程中,会与五位服务人员接触;平均每次接触的短短15秒内,就决定整个公司在乘客心中的印象。故定义:与顾客接触的每一个时间点即为关键时刻,它是从人员的A(Appearance)外表、B(Behavior)行为、C(Communication)沟通三方面来着手。这三方面给人的第一印象所占的比例分别为外表52%、行为33%、沟通15%,是影响顾客忠诚度及满意度的重要因素。
4. Many companies today hire for attitude rather than skill. 当今很多公司在雇用员工的时候往往更看重员工的态度而不是其技能。

Useful Words and Expressions 实用词汇与表达

1. on the outlook 留心
2. be reliant on 依赖,依靠
3. a multitude of 众多的,大批的
4. be particular about 讲究,挑剔
5. at one's convenience 在某人方便的时候
6. attend to 照顾,照料
7. make certain 弄清楚

酒店英语阅读（上）

8. in a timely manner 及时
9. hold onto 紧紧抓住
10. put sb. on hold 把某人晾一边

Practical Reading 实用文体欣赏

ABC Hotel

Policies and Procedures Guide

Cancellations

1. Reservations held on personal credit cards

Reservations guaranteed by personal credit card can be canceled, without penalty, 48 hours prior to the arrival date. Later cancellations will be charged a penalty fee of one night's accommodation. All reservations must be canceled in writing, by e-mail, fax or letter.

2. Reservations booked through travel agencies

Travel agencies will be charged a "late fee" penalty for cancellations. The amount will depend on the reservation terms.

3. Reservations for conference and banquet facilities

A deposit is required to reserve the ABC Hotel's conference/banquet facilities. Deposits will be refunded up to 45 days prior to the scheduled event. The ABC Hotel will charge a "late fee" penalty for cancellations after this date.

Unit 7　Etiquette and Service

Knowledge 趣味小知识

西餐上菜顺序

西餐上菜服务方式有法式、俄式、英式、美式、意式等，各种服务方式既有类似的地方，也有不同之处。酒店通常将几种服务方式混合使用。通常的上菜顺序为：

①头盘：也称为开胃品，一般有冷盘和热头盘之分，常见的品种有鱼子酱、鹅肝酱、熏鲑鱼、鸡尾酒、沙拉、面包和黄油（在开餐前5分钟左右送上）、奶油鸡酥盒、焗蜗牛等。

②汤：大致可分为清汤与浓汤，如牛尾清汤、各式奶油汤、海鲜汤、美式蛤蜊汤、意式蔬菜汤、俄式罗宋汤、法式葱头汤等。

③副菜（中盘）：通常为鱼虾等水产类菜肴与蛋类、酥盒菜肴。

④主菜：多为肉、禽类菜肴或高级海鲜。其中最有代表性的是牛肉或牛排。禽类菜肴的原料取自鸡、鸭、鹅。

⑤蔬菜类菜肴：通常为配菜，可以安排在肉类菜肴之后，也可以与肉类菜肴同时上桌。

⑥甜品：如点心、冰淇淋、奶酪、水果等。

⑦咖啡、茶或餐后酒。

⑧小吃，如曲奇饼等。

西餐餐具语言

西餐就餐时，很多情况不需要开口，客人的一举一动便会告诉服务人员他的意图，而受过训练的服务人员则会按照客人的意愿为其服务，满足其要求，这就是"刀叉语言"。

● 继续用餐：将刀叉分开放，约呈三角形，意为要继续用餐，服务人员将不会收走餐盘。

● 添加饭菜：餐盘已空，但客人仍想用餐，可将刀叉分开放,大约呈八字形,服务人员将再次为其添加饭菜。

• 用餐结束:客人不想继续用餐时,盘空时可将刀叉平行斜放于盘中,约10点钟方向,盘里仍有饭菜时,平行放于盘一边,服务人员则认为客人用餐完毕,会在适当时候将餐盘收走。

Exercises 练习

1. Phrase Translation

1）厨师服
2）仪容仪表
3）贵宾
4）餐桌礼仪
5）服务礼仪
6）all at once
7）cultural norms
8）moments of truth
9）repeat business
10）satisfied customers

2. Passage Translation

Passage A

Be sure to make reservations if the restaurant you chose is a fancy or popular one. It's very embarrassing to show up without reservations and having to wait for a table, leaving a very bad impression on your date. Also, be sure to check to see if they have a dress code and tell your date in advance what to wear. When your food arrives, proper dining etiquette requires you to eat at a moderate pace so that you have time to talk. Don't slurp your soup, smack your lips or chew with your mouth open. Nothing is more unsightly than watching someone talk and chew their food at the same time. If you get food stuck in your mouth, don't pick it out with your fingers or fork at the table. Excuse yourself and go to the restroom and get it out with a toothpick.

Passage B

如果你受邀到一位美国朋友家中晚餐,礼貌起见,请你记住以下几点。首先,准时上门,不要提前。晚10分钟或是15分钟也可以接受,但不要晚45分钟。其次,带一份礼物。鲜花或糖果是永远不会错的。第三,晚餐结束后不要马上离开,但也不要逗留过久。当朋友面露倦意,无话可说的时候,把这当作你要离开的信号。次日,要打个电话或写封感谢信,告诉朋友你昨晚过得非常愉快。

Case Study 案例分析

Disney's Four Basic Service Priorities

The Walt Disney Company, together with its subsidiaries and affiliates, is a leading diversified international family entertainment and media enterprise with five business segments: media networks, parks and resorts, studio entertainment, consumer products and interactive media. The way the Walt Disney Company delivers service at its theme parks and resorts provides some insight into how superior service is delivered consistently. It starts with Disney's four basic service priorities: safety, courtesy, show and efficiency.

Safety is of course a key element, especially in the theme parks, where the potential for accidents is ever-present. If an elderly person with a walker wants to go on the Haunted house ride in the Magic Kingdom, cast members are empowered to stop the ride while the guest is helped onto the walkway. At the same time, a recorded announcement is played for those on the ride: "Ladies and gentlemen, the ghosts and goblins have taken over for a minute." This is just one example of how cast members are trained to handle potential safety problems.

Courtesy is generated by Disney's attitude toward its employees and reinforced by specific training techniques in handling guests. A popular Disney saying is, "Our front line is our bottom line." Disney also believes that guests are always guests, whether they are right or wrong.

The other two service priorities, show (entertainment) and efficiency are obvious throughout the Disney operation. Video monitors, character appearance, and live performances entertain guests during long waits for attractions. Parades, shows and fireworks are used to draw crowds to specific areas of the park. It is easy to tell where to look for a car by asking guests what time they arrived, because specific rows are filled at specific times.

Disney executives estimate that every cast member has 60 moments of truth every day. Clearly, Disney defines quality service as exceeding guest expectations during every one of those encounters. The Disney company helps its cast members exceed guest expectations by paying attention to the smallest details. This meticulous approach pays off, bringing customers back for repeat visits and making Walt Disney World the world's largest single tourist attraction.

Thinking:

1. What are Disney's four basic service priorities?
2. Can you give some other examples on the good service that Disney delivers?

Unit 8　Development and Issues

▶▶ Lead-in 导读

酒店业经过几十年的探索与发展，无论是管理、服务，还是外观设计、硬件设施的投入都得到很大提升。随着IT等高新技术的发展，行业信息化、网络化成为新的趋势，同时，随着地球环境问题的加剧，酒店业环境管理不再是单单一家酒店或是一个集团的行为，而是整个国际酒店产业的行为。本单元从数字化酒店业、绿色酒店、酒店的可持续发展三个角度探讨酒店业的未来发展及所面临的挑战。

Unit 8 Development and Issues

Reading 阅 读

Text A

E-hospitality

What Is E-hospitality①?

The Internet has consolidated itself as a very powerful platform that has changed the way we communicate, and the way we do business. Over the last decade the population of Internet users has increased rapidly. The hospitality industry has always been among the first to capitalize on new technologies.② Customers are constantly seeking new sources of information to help them make decisions before purchasing services. E-hospitality has been defined as "the buying and selling of products and services by hotels and consumers over the Internet."③ With e-hospitality, the landscape of the hospitality industry has forever changed.

The Importance of E-hospitality

Now that each hotel is involved in e-hospitality, why is hotel e-hospitality so important today?

- The Internet is the lowest cost hotel-booking channel
- Most travelers research hotel reservations on the Internet
- Social media and online hotel reviews are an increasingly important decision factor
- The web is the preferred media source for travel information over television, newspapers and magazines

Vocabulary
consolidate *vt.* 巩固，加强
platform *n.* 平台
purchase *v.* 购买

E-hospitality Strategies

Here is a list of the basic e-hospitality strategies that will help to get the best from the Internet world.

- Search-friendly web site design. Site download speed is one of the most important ranking factors in organic search.④

酒店英语阅读（上）

- Improve conversion and usability. With the increasing volume of information that *hoteliers* are trying to provide travelers, it is key for hotels to focus on usability and conversion. It is important to take a *holistic* approach and *prioritize* information. Good web site architecture and organized content improves site usability and its efficiency when used with search engines.

- Mobile. People are using mobile devices to conduct searches, as well as share content, connect with friends and browse the web. Hotels can leverage the mobile market by optimizing their site for mobile phones, improving the download speed of their site by avoiding heavy graphics and Flash, making sure their site is mobile *compatible*, and promoting mobile sites across all platforms including paid, social and local. ⑤

hotelier *n.* 旅馆老板
holistic *adj.* 全盘的，整体的
prioritize *vt.* 按重要性排列
compatible *adj.* 和谐的，协调的

Notes

1. e-hospitality 数字化酒店业。伴随网络的普及，数字化已经渗透到人们日常生活的方方面面。酒店客人的需求也变得越来越数字化，信息、交流、娱乐、办公、旅游等方面越来越离不开数字化。数字化服务，比拼的不仅仅是技术，更是内容。谁能为酒店客人带来更有价值的服务内容，谁就能赢得酒店青睐，并帮助酒店赢得客人。

2. The hospitality industry has always been among the first to capitalize on new technologies. 酒店行业一直是最早利用新技术的行业。

3. E-hospitality has been defined as "the buying and selling of products and services by hotels and consumers over the Internet." 数字化酒店业已经被定义为"酒店和消费者在互联网上购买和销售的产品和服务"。

4. Site download speed is one of the most important ranking factors in organic search. 在有机搜寻中网站下载速度是最重要的因素。有机搜寻（英文：organic search）是描述万维网网站不付费给搜寻引擎做广告而让网站使用者通过搜索引擎"内在"的搜索功能找到该网站的一种方式。有机搜寻不同于点击付费（pay-per-click）广告方式，后者是用付费方式让广告在搜寻结果中突显出来。

5. Hotels can leverage the mobile market by optimizing their site for mobile phones, improving the download speed of their site by avoiding heavy graphics and Flash, making sure their site is mobile compatible, and promoting mobile sites across all platforms including paid, social and local. 酒店可以通过优化手机网站，避免沉重的图形和照片来提高网站的下载速度等方式利用移动市场，确保他们的网站是与移动手机网站兼容的，并促使移动手机网站跨越所有的平台，包括支付平台、交际平台和地方平台。

Unit 8 Development and Issues

Text B

Green and Sustainability

The hotel industry is undergoing many changes. Today, "green" or "sustainable" hotel has become a buzz word① in the Hotel industry.

Going Green

What does being green mean? Although green has become a popular descriptor, it has no standard definition beyond its application to an eco-friendly business. Being green can range from encouraging guests to reuse towels, to recycling waste, to using wind electricity, to cooking with organic foods, to reducing carbon emissions, and to installing rooftop solar panels②. Complying with various benchmarks can result in the application of a green label.

Going green is a big trend today within the hotel industry. Individual hotels and even the headquarters buildings of hotel chains are now being built with environmental concerns in mind. For example, Hilton moved its headquarters during the summer of 2009 from Beverly hills, California, to a new building in Virginia that is LEED③ Gold certified. ("LEED" stands for Leadership in Energy and Environmental Design.)

Green initiatives are in place worldwide, not just in the United States and the rest of North America.

Sustainability

Sustainable development has become one of the most significant issues with regard to hotel development and operations in the past few years. "Sustainable development" was defined in 1987 by the Brundtland Report as "development that meets the needs of the present without compromising the ability of future generations to meet their own needs". ④ Hotel industry in recent past has come up with various sustainable development measures. These measures range from conserving water, and

Vocabulary

descriptor *n.* 描述符
eco-friendly *adj.* 对生态环境友好的
organic *adj.* 有机的
compromise *vt.* 违背(原则)

waste management, to energy saving in order to creating green rooms. Here are a few examples of sustainability policies in hospitality companies.

preserve *vt.* 保护；保持

• Four Seasons Hotels and Resorts are planting 10 million trees around the world.

• Marriott — Spirit to Preserve is the sustainable arm of Marriott's Social Responsibility and Community Engagement program.

• Starwood Hotels and Resorts Worldwide, Inc. — This company has an Environmental Sustainability Policy that outlines the five "green" areas on which they are focused.

Notes

1. buzz word 行话，术语
2. solar panels 太阳能板，太阳能电池板
3. LEED（Leadership in Energy and Environmental Design）是一个评价绿色建筑的工具。它提倡在设计中有效地减少对环境和住户的负面影响。LEED 由美国绿色建筑协会建立并于 2003 年开始推行，在美国部分州和一些国家已被列为法定强制标准。
4. 参见 http://en.wikipedia.org/wiki/Brundtland_Commission. 1987 年世界环境与发展委员会在《我们共同的未来》报告中第一次阐述了可持续发展的概念，得到了国际社会的广泛共识。

Text C

Future Development

The hospitality industry is optimistic and expects a brighter and better trend in coming years. As the economic landscape is progressing, there will be a change in the trend of "staycation,"① and people will intend to focus on the value of travel. In other words, tourists now look for comfortable, simple, yet high-quality experiences. It is important for hospitality companies to capitalize on these opportunities to stay ahead in the industry. Here are some of the emerging trends that people in the hospitality industry should keep in mind while preparing strategies for the future.

• **Hotel Design**. Outside of major urban areas, the future hotel is much more likely to be in environmental harmony with its community. Accommodations will be developed to match their environmental settings, and the local culture will provide inspiration for the design of building features, motifs, furniture, furnishings, and artifacts.② Humanistic scale of buildings and the use of indigenous materials and methods will be more common. This approach will both maximize the economic benefit to be gained by the host community from hotel development, and provide what travelers increasingly want when they seek an experience away from home.

● **Guestrooms.** The hotel guestroom of the future is likely to be better designed and more functional. In appropriate locations, guestrooms will have full office facilities both in the form of work stations and available business equipment. There will be increased emphasis on improved air purification and ventilation systems and improved lighting.③

● **Safety Systems.** With regard to guest safety, litigation and consumer protection trends will influence hotel design and standards. The growing number of female business travelers, in particular, will place a high priority on personal safety. New security equipment (closed-circuit television, keyless door locking systems, and so forth)④ has helped to combat hotel crime. Hotels that have installed such systems, demonstrating a high commitment to guest security, will have an advantage over their competitors who have not.

● **Land Use.** Land scarcity is a growing concern for hotel developers, especially in densely populated cities like London, New York, Tokyo, and Paris. Overall, land shortages in urban centers will force the hotel industry to become more flexible and to seek non-traditional paths to expansion in order to make profitable investments.

● **Mixed-Use Development.** A development approach becoming more prevalent is the combination of hotel development with other real estate projects, frequently referred to as mixed-use realty development⑤ or MXD. These multi-facility developments, particularly common in Hong Kong and Singapore, have begun to spread to Europe, the United States, and elsewhere. For example, new and converted developments that combine retail space, entertainment, offices, and hotel and residential uses are becoming more and more common.

Vocabulary

motif *n.* 主题，基本图案
artifact *n.* 人工制品，手工艺品
humanistic *adj.* 人文主义的
indigenous *adj.* 土生土长的
purification *n.* 提纯
ventilation *n.* 通风设备
litigation *n.* 打官司，诉讼
combat *vt.* 防止，减轻
scarcity *n.* 不足，缺乏
real estate *n.* 不动产，房地产
realty *n.* 不动产，房地产
multi-facility *n.* 多设备

Notes

1. staycation 居家度假
2. Accommodations will be developed to match their environmental settings, and the local culture will provide inspiration for the design of building features, motifs, furniture, furnishings, and artifacts. 未来的酒店将会与周围的环境相融合,地方文化将为酒店在建筑特色、主题设计、家具选择、软装及工艺品设计等方面带来灵感和启发。
3. air purification 空气净化; ventilation systems 通风系统; lighting 照明设备。
4. closed-circuit television 闭路电视; keyless door locking systems 无钥匙门锁系统。
5. mixed-use realty development 多用途的房产开发

Useful Words and Expressions 实用词汇与表达

1. range from...to... 在……到……范围内变化
2. comply with... 服从,遵从
3. result in... 引起,导致
4. with...in mind 记住
5. come up with... 追赶上,比得上
6. focus on... 致力于,使聚焦于
7. keep in mind 记住
8. in harmony with 与……协调,与……一致
9. with regard to 关于
10. be referred to as 被称为……

Practical Reading 实用文体欣赏

ABC HOTEL ENTERTAINMENT REQUEST 宴会申请单	
DATE OF ENTERTAINMENT 宴请日期	ENTERTAINING DEPT 宴请部门
COMPANY TO BE ENTERTAINED 宴请单位	NUMBER OF PERSONES 宴请人数 (including staff member) (包括宴请员工)
STAFF MEMBER 陪同人员	POSITION 职位
REASON FOR ENTERTAINNING 宴请的理由(ATTACH NAME CARDS 附客人名片)	

Unit 8 Development and Issues

PLACE/LOCATION OF ENTERTAINMENT 宴请地点	TIME OF ENTERTAINMENT 宴请时间	
ESTIMATED EXPENSES（RMB）估计费用		
REQUESTED BY 申请人	DEPT.HEAD 部门经理	APPROVED BY GM 总经理批准

Knowledge 趣味小知识

零点菜单

根据不同的价格形式，菜单可分成零点菜单、套菜菜单和混合式菜单三种类型。其中，零点菜单是最常见、使用最广泛的一种菜单形式，其特点是菜单的每一道菜式都标明价格。零点菜单可以是早餐菜单，也可以是午餐、晚餐菜单，或者是特种菜单或客房餐饮菜单，等等。零点菜单的价格档次多样，能迎合不同层次的宾客需求。零点菜单不但适用于一般社会餐馆，而且同样适用于旅游饭店的各类正餐厅、风味餐厅、咖啡厅等。

冷餐会

自助餐（buffet），有时亦称冷餐会，它是目前国际上所通行的一种非正式的西式宴会，在大型商务活动中尤为多见。其具体做法是，不预备正餐，由就餐者在用餐时自行选择食物、饮料，自由地与他人在一起或是独自一人用餐。

自助餐，是起源于西餐的一种就餐方式。厨师将烹制好的冷、热菜肴及点心陈列在餐厅的长条桌上，由客人自己随意取食，自我服务。这种就餐形式起源于公元8—11世纪北欧的"斯堪的纳维亚式餐前冷食"和"亨联早餐（Hunt breakfast）"。

自助餐之所以被叫作冷餐会，主要是因其提供的食物以冷食为主。当然，适量地提供一些热菜，或者提供一些半成品由用餐者自己进行加工，也是允许的。

Exercises 练习

1. Phrase Translation

1) 入住天数
2) 折扣优惠
3) 行政楼层
4) 豪华间
5) 海景房
6) a wake-up call
7) block off
8) ground floor
9) high season
10) free parking

2. Passage Translation

Passage A

Sustainability will become a very important issue for the hospitality industry in the following years. Rising populations and increasingly scarce resources will provide a challenging business environment in which sustainability will need to be embedded within all facets of the hospitality industry. Future business leaders must be able to balance ecologic, economic, and social concerns, which are most commonly known as the triple bottom line. Uneconomical growth is growth that depletes the ecosystem resulting in a declined quality of life. Conservation techniques such as waste reduction and energy efficacy, reduce costs, liability insurance, environmental penalties, and disposable costs, may lead to an increase in market share from an improved public image.

Passage B

客人入住酒店时应注意以下9点：1)永远不要对酒店员工大喊大叫；2)不要告诉任何人你的房间号；3)如果酒店员工没佩戴身份证件，不要让他进入你的房间；4)不要指责酒店员工偷了你的东西，一般来说，客人报告的被偷物件99%都能在其房间里找到；5)如果发现客房送餐服务菜单有污损，那就不要点餐；6)如果已经是春季了，而菜单上还写着"冬季菜单"，不要点餐；7)不要用浴室的毛巾来卸妆或是擦鞋；8)不要滥用延时退房特权，如果你确实需要下午1点以后退房，去找经理谈；9)不要将无人看管的行李留在酒店大堂。

Case Study 案例分析

Starwood Hotel

Profile:

A leading worldwide Hotel, Resort & Timeshare company with respected brands including Westin, Sheraton, W, St. Regis and Le Meridien. Starwood today operates over 900 hotel properties covering all continents.

Challenge/Opportunity:

Initially begun as a real-estate investment company, in 2000 Starwood needed to become a top-notch operator of hotels with diverse brands and histories. The goal: Build a consistent, customer-driven culture across the company, and create a consistent guest experience while meeting individual needs and preferences. Increase competitiveness and drive growth in spite of a challenging travel environment.

Pivotal Services and Solutions:

• Conduct extensive research & planning to develop a business case for a "Six Sigma" initiative and plan complex, aggressive global deployment;

• Advise and train corporate executives and hotel leaders worldwide, supporting project selection and integration of improvement practices into ongoing operations;

• Develop and provide license to multi-level training and support materials;

• Coach and training "Belts" of all types, beginning with a high-volume global roll-out with continuing efforts through today.

Results/Successes:

Starwood credits this effort with not only significant ROI through both savings and increased revenue—the company enjoys a higher net margin than its key competitors—but also with helping spark and act on innovative ideas. The impact is based on a global culture: most ideas and solutions come from hotel staff throughout the world.

Thinking:

1. What is the goal of Starwood?
2. What is the global culture of Starwood Hotels?

练习参考答案

Unit 1

1. Phrase Translation

1) all-suite hotel
2) full-service hotel
3) business hotel
4) general manager
5) management trainee
6) 葡萄酒酒标
7) 零点餐
8) 延时居住酒店
9) 初级职位
10) 起伏

2. Passage Translation

Passage A

旅游接待业是当今世界最大的行业,也是最具活力的行业之一。这个行业的发展日新月异、激动人心,提供了无限可能。旅游接待业需要大量多层次的人才,既需要具有商业头脑的人才,也需要具有艺术创造力的人才。这个行业可以让你充分发展自己的技能和兴趣,从而找到适合自己的位置。由于其业务范围广泛,专业方向众多,你可以在业内轻松改变工作领域。你可以随着兴趣的变化和增加而改变发展方向,追逐新的潮流,抓住新的机会,赶上科技的快速发展,这一切都灵活自如。你也可以运用自己的专长,创办自己的公司或推出独家经营理念。

Passage B

The 1980's saw the beginnings of China's hotel transformation, probably best illustrated by the well-known Jianguo Hotel. It was the first Sino-foreign joint venture hotel, opening in

1982 and operated by the Peninsula Hotel Group. Other notable hotels built at the time were Beijing's Great Dragon Hotel, a five-star property donated to China by Hong Kong's shipping magnate Sir Y K Pao (Bao Yu Gang). Significantly, Deng Xiao Ping attended the grand opening ceremony and inscribed the name of the hotel in Chinese calligraphy.

Unit 2

1. Phrase Translation

1) target market
2) guest satisfaction
3) second and third-tier cities
4) pay-as-you-view TV
5) market share
6) 性能比
7) 临时旅店
8) 采购成本
9) 预算节约型旅客
10) 购物商场

2. Passage Translation

Passage A

会议型酒店的客房数量通常在350间到2000间不等，并且配以充足的公共空间和会议设施。先进的视听和通信技术以及大规模的餐饮设施是会议型酒店必须具备的。与传统酒店相比，新型的会议型酒店往往拥有双倍空间的会议室，公共空间也很开阔，便于办理团体入住登记。会议型酒店在人流管理上也不同于传统的普通酒店。例如：散客入住登记和会议客人入住登记的区域是分开的，这不仅在一定程度上提高了工作效率，而且减少了大堂内的噪音和拥挤程度。同样，散客和会议客人的泊车区域也是分开的。

Passage B

A timeshare hotel is a property with a particular form of use rights. These properties are typically hotel rooms or resort condominium units. Their use rights have been subdivided into a number of weeks, are sold to different customers in form of membership, according to 10 to 40 years or even longer time. Each sharer is allotted 7 days each year in which they may use the property. The sharers can exchange their room's use rights with the counterparts in other areas by means of exchanging service system, to lower the cost of travel in different areas.

Unit 3

1. Phrase Translation

1) undersea resort
2) marine life
3) art gallery
4) make full use of
5) recycled materials
6) 连接到
7) 与……互动
8) 住店客人
9) 瞥见
10) 充分地

2. Passage Translation

Passage A

Kelebek 在土耳其语中意为"蝴蝶",之所以如此叫它,是因为它有两个精灵般的烟囱从岩石中耸立出来,像极蝴蝶的两个翅膀。蝴蝶洞穴酒店坐落于神秘的卡帕多奇亚,形成酒店的岩层可追溯到史前的火山喷发时期。几千年来,这里的人们一直居住在这些洞穴之中。最早提到卡帕多奇亚洞穴村落的是一本著作于公元前6世纪的波斯文献,而"卡帕多奇亚"一名的文字记载则由第一位历史学家希罗多德提及。入住蝴蝶酒店能让您体验到卡帕多奇亚人传统洞穴住所的独特内部景致。您可以选择一间中世纪僧侣曾经居住的房间,也可以选择布满古老镶嵌图案的房间。蝴蝶洞穴酒店拥有您想要的一切现代便利设施,您可以尽情享受在此的每一天,探索这块迷人的土地!

Passage B

Through years, an American couple Dennis and Frances, both are chainsaw artists, has put up an unusual Dog Bark Park Inn, which accommodates travelers with beds and breakfast. Not only the construction appearance, but also the interior furnishings and the food of the hotel are made into dog shape. Dog Bark Park is located in the central part of Camas Prairie, Idaho. Now, there are two huge "Beagles" sitting on the green in the park. One is called "Sweet Willy", which is 30 feets high and completed in 1997; the other one is named "Toby" with 12 feets high. At the beginning, they just wanted to build the park, which was assumed to be a place for making, displaying and selling chainsaw carvings. But later, they came to the idea of making two big "Beagles" and producing works around the theme of dog. The Dog Bark Park Inn is favored by many dog lovers. The guests attracted to be here can access to the "body" of the Beagles through a "secret stairs", and there are cookies of dog shape in every room. It is really fascinating!

Unit 4

1. Phrase Translation

1) hotel rating system
2) hotel lobby
3) advance notice
4) guest experience
5) service quality
6) 中等偏上
7) 酒店设施
8) 价格合理
9) 洗衣机
10) 公共交通

2. Passage Translation

Passage A

不同于传统的星级酒店，精品酒店更强调个性化。成功的精品酒店一般具有三个特点，即独立精神、个性特征以及文化遗产。总体而言，精品酒店拥有丰富的地域文化特色和独特的历史特征。精品酒店能够给客人带来无与伦比的享受，而这一点正是星级酒店所欠缺的。四合院，是古代中国人用于居住的典型的四方形建筑，它是中国独有的一种建筑形式。四合院由正房和东西厢房组成。近年来，已经有越来越多的四合院改造成酒店，用于接待来自世界各地的游客。四合院展现了东方古典建筑之美，在这里，客人不仅可以感受传统的气息，还可以了解更多的中国历史。

Passage B

China National Tourism Administration (CNTA in short) is an agency in charge of tourism directly affiliated to the State Council. The main responsibilities of the CNTA are: Planning and coordinating the development of the tourism industry, preparing development policies, programs and standards, drafting up relevant laws and regulations and supervising the implementation, as well as guiding regional tourism. Establishing and organizing the implementation of market development strategies for domestic tourism, inbound tourism and outbound tourism, organizing external publicity and significant promotional activities on the overall image of China's tourism. Promoting the international communication and cooperation of tourism and taking charge of affairs relating to the cooperation with international tourist organizations. Establishing policies on outbound tourism and border tourism and organizing the implementation. Examining and approving foreign travel agencies established in China, examining the market access qualifications of foreign-invested travel agencies and travel agencies engaged in international tourism, examining and approving overseas (outbound) tourism and border tourism cases.

Unit 5

1. Phrase Translation

1) room inventory
2) time zone
3) business and leisure travelers
4) cater to
5) stand out
6) 定下基调
7) 以……为自豪
8) 延住客人
9) 做出抉择
10) 商业枢纽,商业中心

2. Passage Translation

Passage A

凯宾斯基的目标是成为知名饭店品牌,提供欧式经典奢华体验。我们为寻求完美和个性化的客人提供服务。指引我们一路走来的发展战略是长期的,它注重我们的企业价值。

凯宾斯基以为追求卓越、注重个性的客人提供服务为宗旨。凯宾斯基未公开上市,仍是一家承蒙股东支持的私有企业,这意味着我们能够专注于长期发展战略,创造可持续发展的价值。我们相信,通过分权方式,我们定能完美实现凯宾斯基的品牌承诺,提供欧式经典的奢华体验。我们充分信赖、授权各区域分支的员工,确保能够提供独一无二的品牌承诺,并体现各个地区、国家和酒店独特的文化。

Passage B

HYATT is a global hospitality company with widely recognized, industry leading brands and a tradition of innovation developed over our more than fifty-year history. Our mission is to provide authentic hospitality by making a difference in the lives of the people we touch every day. We focus on this mission in pursuit of our goal of becoming the most preferred brand in each segment that we serve for our associates, guests, and owners. We support our mission and goal by adhering to a set of core values that characterizes our culture.

Unit 6

1. Phrase Translation

1) chain hotels
2) occupancy levels
3) room rate
4) concierge service
5) room service
6) 半膳宿服务
7) 未经预约的客人
8) 相邻房
9) 点心
10) 擦去灰尘

2. Passage Translation

Passage A

瑞士酒店管理教育集团(SEG)自1982年建立第一所酒店学校以来,已发展成为全球领先的酒店管理教育集团。SEG所取得的成就令人瞩目,它已成为行业标杆,不断鼓舞着所有毕业生。SEG成员学校全部由瑞士创建和管理,保证学生获得带有独特瑞士风格的高品质教育，这种教育风格世界闻名。SEG拥有真正的国际化教育环境：校园内的学生来自全世界八十多个国家，实操型教学与理论教学相结合，专注培养符合酒店业需求的人才。瑞士酒店管理教育集团旗下的五所大学是：恺撒里兹酒店管理大学、库林那美食艺术管理大学、蒙特勒酒店工商管理大学、纳沙泰尔酒店管理大学、瑞士酒店管理大学。

Passage B

Message of Welcome

Dear Guest:

Welcome to ABC Hotel!

All of us are very grateful for your patronage and hope you enjoy your stay at our hotel. This *Service Directory* will inform you various service and facilities of our hotel. If you need more help, please contact with our relevant departments, all of us already stand by and surely you will get the excellent service at any time.

You are our first concern in ABC Hotel during your stay. We shall try our best to offer the perfect service for you. If there are any more comments or suggestions, please contact us promptly or fill in questionnaire form on the desk of your room.

We wish a pleasant stay with us and we hope we will have the pleasure of serving you again.

ABC Hotel
General Manager

Unit 7

1. Phrase Translation

1) chef coats
2) physical appearance
3) guest of honor
4) table manners
5) service etiquette
6) 同时，一起
7) 文化标准
8) 关键时刻

9) 回头生意

10) 满意的顾客

2. Passage Translation

Passage A

如果你选择的是一家高档或很受欢迎的餐馆,一定要提前预订。如果未预订就去了,到时候没有桌子得等上半天,将非常尴尬,而且还会给约会对象留下不好的印象。此外,一定要打听一下餐馆对着装有无要求,要事先告诉对方应穿什么样的衣服。饭菜端上来时,要用餐得体,吃东西不能过快或过慢,这样你才有时间和对方交流。喝汤不要出声、吧唧嘴,或张着嘴巴嚼东西。没有什么比看着一个边嚼东西边说话的人更不雅观的了。如果有东西塞在嘴里,不要在饭桌上用手指或叉子挑出来。要请对方原谅后到洗手间用牙签将东西挑出来。

Passage B

If you're invited to an American friend's home for dinner, keep in mind these rules for polite behavior. First of all, arrive approximately on time, but not early. It's OK to be ten or fifteen minutes late but not forty-five minutes late. Secondly, it's polite to bring a small gift. Flowers or candy are always appropriate. Last, don't leave immediately after dinner, but don't overstay, either. When your friends seem to be getting tired and running out of conversation, take their behavior as a cue to leave. The next day, call or write a thank-you note to say how much you enjoyed the evening.

Unit 8

1. Phrase Translation

1) length of stay

2) bulk discount

3) executive floor

4) deluxe room

5) sea view room

6) 叫醒电话

7) 封闭,封锁

8) 底层

9) 旺季

10) 免费停车

2. Passage Translation

Passage A

未来几年,可持续发展将成为旅游接待业一个非常重要的问题。人口的不断增长和日益稀缺的资源将使旅游接待业面临巨大的挑战,旅游接待业的方方面面都必须认真思考可持续发展问题。未来的业界领导人必须能够平衡好被称为"三重底线"的生态、经济和社会发展问题。低效增长是使生态系统枯竭而导致生活质量下降的增长方式。一些节能措施,如减少废物、降低能耗、节约成本、实行责任保险、实施破坏环境处罚等将提升企业公众形象,从而增加市场份额。

Passage B

Guests should pay attention to nine details at the hotel:

1) Don't yell at the staff ever;

2) Don't tell anyone your room number;

3) Don't let a hotel employee into your room if they do not have an I.D.;

4) Don't blame hotel staff for stealing your stuff—the guests eventually find 99% of the items that guests report stolen from their rooms;

5) Don't order from room service if you notice the pages are dirty and torn;

6) Don't order if the menu reads "Winter Menu" when it's spring;

7) Don't use the bathroom washcloths to take off your makeup or shine your shoes;

8) Don't abuse the privilege of late checkout—If you really need one past 1:00 p.m., ask for the manager;

9) Don't leave your luggage unattended in a hotel lobby.

参考书目

Chuck Y. Gee. *International Hotels Development and Management*. Lansing, Mich.: American Hotel & Lodging Educational Institute, 2008.

Chuck Y. Gee. *Resorts Development and Management* (Second Edition). Lansing, Mich.: The Educational Institute of the American Hotel & Lodging Association, 1988.

Chuck Y. Gee. *World of Resorts from Development to Management* (Third Edition). Lansing, Mich.: American Hotel & Lodging Educational Institute, 2010.

David K. Hayes, Jack Ninemeier. *Hotel Operations Management* (Second Edition). Upper Saddle River: Pearson Education, Inc., 2007.

Debra F. Cannon, Catherine M. Gustafson. *Training and Development for the Hospitality Industry*. Lansing, Mich.: The Educational Institute of the American Hotel & Lodging Association, 2002.

Debra F. Cannon, Catherine M. Gustafson. *Training and Development for the Hospitality Iindustry*. Lansing, Mich.: The Educational Institute of the American Hotel & Lodging Association, 2002.

Dennis J. Cahill. *How Consumers Pick a Hotel: Strategic Segmentation and Target Marketing*. Albany: Delmar, 1999.

Ismail, Ahmed. *Hotel Sales & Operations*. Albany: Delmar, 1999.

J. R. Tewari. *Hotel Front Office: Operations and Management*. New Delhi: OUP India, 2009.

J. Stephen Sarazen, James M. Salter. *Managing the Customer Satisfaction Process*. United States: American Management Association, 1993.

Marvin Cetron, Fred DeMicco, Owen Davies. *Hospitality 2015: the Future of Hospitality and Travela*. Lansing Mich.: American Hotel & Lodging Educational Institute, 2010.

Matt A. Casado. *Housekeeping Management*. Hoboken: Wiley Publishing Inc, 2011.

McDowell Bryson, Adele Ziminski. *The Concierge: Key to Hospitality*. New Jersey: Wiley, 1992.

Michael L. Kasavana, Richard M. Brooks. *Managing Front Office Operations*. Lansing, Mich.: The Educational Institute of American Hotel & Lodging Association, 2005.

Raymond Cote. *Accounting for Hospitality Managers*. Lansing, Mich.: The Educational Institute of the American Hotel & Motel Association, 2001.

Robert H. Woods, Misty M. Johanson, Michael P. Sciarini. *Managing Hospitality Human Resource*. Lansing, Mich.: The Educational Institute of the American Hotel & Lodging, 2012.

Rocco M. Angelo, Andrew N. Vladimir. *Hospitality Today: An Introduction (Sixth Edition)*. Lansing,

Mich.: The Educational Institute of the American Hotel & Lodging Association, 2007.
Tom Baum. *Hospitality Management*. Thousand Oaks: SAGE Publications Ltd, 2011.
Walker, John R. *Introduction to Hospitality* (Fourth Edition). Upper Saddle River: Pearson Education, Inc., 2006.

雷明化、葛华平主编:《客房服务与管理》,北京:中国人民大学出版社,2013年。
张志军:《饭店安全管理实务》,北京:旅游教育出版社,2008年。
http://www.ahla.com
http://www.ehow.com
http://www.hospitalitynet.org
http://www.hoteldeglace-canada.com
http://hotel-industry.learnhub.com
http://www.hotel-online.com
http://www.knowledgeatwharton.com.cn
http://www.poseidonresorts.com
http://www.sourcesecurity.com/tags/hotel-security.html
http://www.safety-security-crazy.com/hotel-safety.html
http://www.securityandsafety.co.uk/main7.htm
http://www.travelchinaguide.com/hotel/rate.asp
http://www.uichlesclefsdor.org
http://www.visitbritain.com/zh/CN
http://www.wisegeek.com
http://www.whitepod.com
http://en.wikipedia.org/wiki/Hotel_rating
中国网:http://www.china.org.cn
香格里拉酒店集团官网:http://www.shangri-la.com
洲际酒店集团官网:http://www.ihg.com
希尔顿酒店集团官网:http://www3.hilton.com
康奈尔大学官网:http://www.cornell.edu
洛桑酒店管理学院官网:http://www.ehl.edu/eng
格里昂酒店管理学院官网:http://www.glion.edu
天津财经大学教学资源:http://jpkc.tjufe.edu.cn/2010/fandian/glal.htm
中国期刊网:http://www.chinaqking.com/hw/2007/4483.html